RIDING FEAR FREE

RIDING FEAR FREE

Help for Fearful Riders and Their Teachers

LAURA DALEY
and
JENNIFER BECTON

WHITELEY PRESS, LLC

WHITELEY PRESS, LLC
www.bectonliterary.com

What Trainers Are Saying about
Riding Fear Free

Normally, I don't read books like *Riding Fear Free*. It's not that I haven't had fear issues with riding, but I'm just not into self-help books. Once I started reading *Riding Fear Free*, I found that I didn't want to put it down! I was enlightened by the process, and it gave me new insight to what my clients go through. I have already incorporated some of the ideas in dealing with fearful clients. This book has amazing potential to help many people.
— Raye Lochert, Trainer, Raye Lochert Horsemanship

Riding Fear Free is a valuable resource for any horse owner. After reading *Riding Fear Free*..., I have a newfound respect for what [fearful riders] were going through. *Riding Fear Free* has given me the knowledge I need to patiently and respectfully help others become fear free.
— Josh Rushing, Professional Horsemen, 2010 EXCA World Champion

Riding Fear Free is going to help so many people to overcome their fear and to not feel so alone. This book will help them.
— Brandi Lyons, Trainer, No Limits Horsemanship

The science behind [*Riding Fear Free*]...made addressing the fear as an issue itself as legitimate and important as what I always thought of as the "real" lesson. This is required reading for any instructor.
— Blaine Rankin, Level 4 CHA Certified Instructor

[*Riding Fear Free*] helped me to see my students in a new and hopefully, a more empowering way.
— Kim Robatille, Trainer, Two Minds One Ride

I recommended [*Riding Fear Free*] to one of my clients, and she got a lot out of it.
— Charles Wilhelm, Trainer, Charles Wilhelm Training Center

[*Riding Fear Free*] is the book I've been waiting for — without even knowing it. Trying to help riders with fears I often didn't understand was frustrating. And there just wasn't much help out there for fearful riders or those working with them — until now. These authors truly understand the various types of fear and most importantly commonsense, simple ways to fix them
— Kathy Huggins, Owner, Cedar Creek Training Stables

What Riders Are Saying about
Riding Fear Free

I happened upon [*Riding Fear Free*] by accident and was pretty skeptical. I skimmed the book and found some interesting things that I decided to try, and was I ever surprised by the difference in my fear level. I was trapped by the negative thoughts and images in my mind, but no more! I truly am *Riding Fear Free*!
— Jenny Zogg

[*Riding Fear Free*] forced me to re-think how I view fear, in myself and in others, and how to react to it. I believe my daughter's riding experience would have been much different if I had read this book ten years ago. I would highly recommend this book to everyone who has any fear or deals with people who may be fearful. Parents, riding instructors, spouses and those who ride with fearful partners would all benefit greatly from reading this book.
— DeborahLynn Sherwood

Riding Fear Free gave me steps to take that built my confidence and riding ability. The progressive, small steps the book encourages as well as the techniques such as journaling and short rides has made good horsemanship an obtainable goal.
— Jen Hooker

I have spent the past year working my way through the [*Riding Fear Free*] process. One day everything clicked, and I took the next step up into the saddle. It was a fifteen-minute ride that felt like old times. I have ridden since and feel the confidence growing with each one as my enjoyment returns.
— Joy Senger

Riding Fear Free is more than amazing! It is life-changing. I tried it all-the traditional advice to "just do it," reading anything I could find on the subject, watching training shows, reading self-help books, etc.... Nothing had the answers I was searching for. And then, one blessed day, I found the one! Laura Daley and Jennifer Becton have researched and written a guide to put fearful riders back in the saddle in a manner unlike any I have experienced before. This is a must read for anyone experiencing horse-related fear, no matter what the cause. You will not regret it!
— Jennifer Woodruff

This book is dedicated to our families
Dave, Sean, and Tyler Daley
and
Bert Becton
and to our perfect horses
Im Aneat (Anita)
and
Call Me Crazy (Darcy),
and it was made possible only through the grace of God.

Table of Contents

Part 1
The Basics: Fear and Fear-free Riding

Part 2
Beyond the Basics

I have the passion to learn to ride, but fear has been a huge obstacle for me. I have never had a wreck or been hurt by a horse. I have the best trainer—my husband John Lyons—available to me 24/7 and the best trained horses to work with, and yet my fear takes over. I have cried, prayed, and beaten myself up plenty for not being better at riding. Many people ask with disbelief in their voices, "What? You're married to John Lyons and are afraid? What is wrong with you?" Or they say, "You could ride my horse. He's the best trained horse ever!" But it doesn't matter how skilled the horse trainer is or how well the horse is trained, I am still afraid I am going to get hurt.

But there is someone out there who really understands what I go through in trying to learn to ride, so it is such an honor for me to have been asked to write the foreword for *Riding Fear Free: Help for Fearful Riders and Their Teachers*. Laura Daley and Jennifer Becton have absolutely nailed the topic of fear from a scientific perspective and given me real techniques for managing it in the saddle and around my horse Charlie. This book gave me hope.

I carried the manuscript around with me for two weeks and read parts of it when I could. I couldn't put it down. In fact, I found myself thinking about it most of the day. I have already started to use Laura and Jennifer's principles myself. For the first time, I am excited about going to the barn and spending time with Charlie, and I love to visualize myself taking perfect, fear-free rides. Riding Fear Free has given me the confidence I needed just to start somewhere, to realize that wherever I start is okay, and to know that I can—and should—walk away if I become scared.

I met Laura Daley and her two handsome boys about twelve years ago at the Western States Horse Expo in Sacramento, California, where John and I had a booth. Laura's enthusiasm, kindness, and love of her boys, horses, and helping others shined through her. Even though I knew what a special lady she is, I am in awe at the magnitude of her understanding of the fearful rider and her knowledge of how to help them. The inclusion of Jennifer's research helped explain what was happening from a scientific perspective, and I am impressed by the book they have written together. Honestly, I have never met anyone with their level of understanding on the topic.

Riding Fear Free has truly given me hope of one day being fear free, and I know this book will help many teachers and students. I am so thankful for the two ladies who have taken the time to write it. I would highly recommend *Riding Fear Free* to anyone. In fact, John Lyons is going to read this book and learn the principles also. Even though he is already a great trainer, this information will help him understand where the fearful riding is coming from and why. Meanwhile, I am excited to work with Laura and my horse Charlie so that I can learn to ride fear free too.

Jody Lyons
July 2012
JohnLyons.biz

Introduction by Laura Daley

Some people say I was born to work with horses and to teach children. Growing up surrounded by both, it was a natural progression. I have always had a passion to help other people, children and adults. I believe this desire is a gift from God, and without that foundation, I could not have developed these techniques or had any success with my clients and students over the past thirty years.

I grew up on a large-scale Arabian breeding ranch and have spent my entire life learning about horses. My first horse-training experiences came as a child, but I never stopped learning. As an adult, I became a Brandi Lyons Certified trainer. I firmly believe in continued education and shared experiences, and I often attend clinics with respected trainers such as Brandi Lyons, Pat Parelli, Richard Shrake, Ken McNabb, Raye Lochert, Julie Goodnight, and John and Josh Lyons. In addition to my horse training experience, I study and practice natural hoof care, equine massage, and chiropractic care. I believe in and merge conditioned-response training methods with physical therapies to create a balanced, peaceful, and willing equine partner.

But I'm not just a trainer of horses. I'm also a teacher of riders. I became a registered Professional Association of Therapeutic Horsemanship International (PATH) riding instructor in 1997 and have studied the methods of Sally Swift, who pioneered Centered Riding techniques, and Eckart Meyners, a German dressage and body awareness teacher. I am a veteran 4H leader and teacher of underprivileged youth and special needs clients. Physically challenged riders have a special place in my heart. I have had arthritis in my ankles since I was seventeen, so that has given me a unique and personal insight into the struggle to overcome physical hardships and pain.

My specialty is helping fearful riders overcome their fears. Using techniques that I have developed over a lifetime of teaching, I have helped hundreds of once-fearful people become fear free. I combine the same conditioned-response methods I use on horses with techniques that help riders accept and take control of their emotions in healthy and safe ways.

A Note to Fearful Riders

I hope you read this book with an open heart and that it helps you become the fear-free rider you dream you could be. You have started on an amazing journey. Like any long journey, there are a lot of twists and turns, rabbit trails, and even road blocks, but you can do it, and we are here to help. I am proud of you for choosing to stop living with your fear. My prayer for you is complete peace.

A Note to Teachers

Thank you for reading this book. Whether you picked it up yourself or one of your students has asked you to read it, you are to be commended for putting your students first in this process. It is obvious that you have a great passion for teaching and willingness to keep learning. *Riding Fear Free* presents ideas that differ greatly from the ways most trainers and riding instructors have dealt with fearful riders. In order to help fearful—and not just slightly unconfident—riders, you may need to change some of your teaching habits and maybe some of your core beliefs about fear. You are not required to take on fearful riders as students if that is not truly what you want to do. Not all teachers want to delve into this area, and that's okay. Be honest about your interests, and then relay the truth to the prospective student.

Thanks again for taking the time to read this book.

I am a fearful rider.

Actually, I am a fearful rider in recovery.

Even as a horse-crazy child, I was never a particularly bold rider. I never got to experience those carefree childhood days in the saddle when nothing was scary and everything was magical. I was always too aware of the vast size and power gap between me and even the smallest, most ancient lesson pony. As an adult rider, I took dressage lessons and grew tremendously from them. Still, I remained timid, and then a runaway incident made my fear nearly unmanageable.

My friend, a dressage instructor and trusted judge of horses, and I were looking for my first horse, and I was having one final canter on a lovely prospect, a warmblood cross, when suddenly we were flying around the arena at a full gallop. I literally froze in terror. My arms and legs would not move. My friend shouted at me, trying to get me to use the outside rein, keeping the horse on the rail to avoid having him take me unwillingly over the jumps that dotted the center of the arena. I managed to keep him away from the jumps, but other than keeping a tight outside rein, I was just a passenger as we galloped madly around and around.

Finally, the horse's owner, who had given us privacy to bond, rushed out of the barn and leapt in front of the horse. In that instant, my life did not flash before my eyes, though that's what I expected. Instead, as I saw her position herself in front of us, I mentally composed my obituary: "Rider killed by crazy horse; owner injured in the accident." The horse jumped sideways to avoid his owner, and the whole affair ended with my face in the gravel driveway and a hoof grazing my helmet. I was never so happy to see gravel in my life. Or that I had worn my helmet.

After the runaway, my fear rose to a new level. Everything about horseback riding was terrifying, even skills I knew well. Still, I managed to purchase my first horse: a National Show Horse (Arab x Saddlebred) mare with the registered name Call Me Crazy. And I really felt like people should be calling me crazy. I was almost too terrified to ride the horse I'd waited twenty years to own. Forget trotting a twenty-meter circle. I was fighting to let someone lead me around at the walk for five minutes. And my terror was rubbing off on my new horse, whom I called Darcy. She became increasingly nervous, so I became even more terrified. We were on a definite downward spiral.

I couldn't even handle taking my usual weekly dressage lesson on Darcy, so I decided it was time to hire a professional trainer to help us out of the spiral of fear. I chose a John Lyons certified trainer because John seemed to be the most well versed of the big-name trainers in dealing with fearful riders. He often says that "fear is common sense in disguise," and his policy is to "ride where you can and not where you can't" (*Fear in the Rider*). And after various well-meaning people had advised me just to grit my teeth through it or take a gallop in the pasture to meet the fear head on, being told that my fear was keeping me safe and to ride only where I felt comfortable appealed to me.

Our Lyons-certified trainer worked miracles for Darcy and me, but our time with him ended before I was able to address my biggest fear: cantering. My horse was now soft on the bridle, responsive, and happier, and my fear had diminished greatly, but it was still there, waiting below the surface. In the intervening years, I hired other wonderful trainers to help us. Each one filled in another piece of the fear puzzle, and my confidence grew, but I still had not accomplished my dream of cantering in a pasture.

Then, I met Laura Daley, a Brandi-Lyons certified trainer and a horsewoman with more than thirty years of experience training horses and helping fearful riders. Actually, I had known her for years through an online discussion board, but she approached me about editing her book of inspirational horse stories, and in exchange, she told me that she would help me become a fear-free rider.

I was skeptical.

I had done all the traditional things to help me overcome fear. I took riding lessons on good horses. I was fit and balanced. I wore a helmet. I sought training for my horse and created a trusting bond with her. I figured I was naturally more fearful than most people, and I would just have to live with it. I would never canter in a field.

"No," Laura said, "it doesn't have to be that way." I could truly be a fear-free rider.

I didn't know how it would be possible for her to help me, especially because she lives on the West Coast and I live on the East Coast, but I thought, "What the heck! Let's give it a try." I had nothing to lose and everything to gain.

What resulted from our relationship has been nothing short of life-altering. After researching and confirming the science behind the techniques Laura suggested, I ended up following her advice. I wrote pages of journal entries and cried lots of tears. I did visualization exercises while riding my "Virtual Darcy," an exercise ball, and I rode the real Darcy while learning to ask good questions about what was happening to cause my anxiety.

After less than one year, I cantered three steps down the barn's driveway without fear. Then, I fulfilled my dream of cantering a few steps in a pasture, but this was just the beginning of my journey to cantering

fear free. These first canters happened in a completely natural way because they grew out of the work I had done all year. I had become fear free and I didn't even realize it. And I did it all through email and a few phone conversations with Laura.

Fortunately for me, Laura also came all the way across the country to help me take my fear-free riding to the next level. We also began our work on this book, which evolved out of the need we saw in the horse community and the lack of in-depth material to help fearful riders. During our week together, I got to experience Laura's techniques in person. I had so many "light-bulb" moments, I probably could have powered the lights at Turner Field. By the time Laura left, I hooked up my trailer, loaded Darcy from five feet away, drove to a local trail-riding facility, and had my first canter at a new place with no fences and no fear.

After experiencing the freedom, magic, and joy of riding fear free, I wanted to share those feelings with others, and because I am a writer, editor, and publisher, a book was my first thought. Since most of what I accomplished came through the written word, I felt that others too could benefit from a book that details Laura's techniques. Although this book also includes the sound, traditional advice that fearful riders often receive, Laura's techniques transcend these basics and offer a path for those who are willing and ready to change and become truly fear free.

Laura and Jennifer at Camp Daley 2010.

How to Use This Book

Riding Fear Free is meant to be an interactive, inspirational tool, and it is best used in conjunction with a journal. Before you read further, grab a pen or open a blank document on your computer, and get ready for your journey to riding fear free. As you read, record the ideas, memories, or thoughts that come to you, and consider taking your notes to the barn as you process your experiences. The sooner you start noticing and recording your emotions, ideas, and thoughts, the sooner you will ride fear free.

How This Book Is Organized

Riding Fear Free is divided into two main parts—"The Basics" and "Beyond the Basics"—and many chapters offer tips tailored to fearful riders ("Rider Tips") and to those who work with them ("Teacher Tips").

Part 1, "The Basics: Fear and Fear-free Riding," provides a brief overview of what fear is and how the brain overcomes it. It also details common advice given to fearful riders and attempts to show why more focused attention on the rider's emotions can help a person deal with horse-related fear once and for all.

Part 2, "Beyond the Basics," deals with general principles, methods, and exercises that go beyond the common advice given to fearful riders. Each technique is based on the scientific concept of fear extinction through conditioned response and memory replacement.

Rather than providing step-by-step lesson plans in an attempt to foresee all possible training needs, this second section of *Riding Fear Free* offers exercises and techniques that can be learned and applied as the rider requires. Once understood, riders can apply major concepts—replacing memories, dealing with emotions, asking good questions/seeing reality, visualizing and distracting, and journal-keeping—in any given situation, from first contact with the horse to cross-country jumping.

In addition, this book contains one chapter specifically from a rider's perspective and one from the teacher's perspective, and each deals with topics unique to that specific role. Riders without a trainer or instructor should consider reading both the rider and teacher sections.

Even though *Riding Fear Free* is designed to help people overcome fear, the exercises will never push riders to the point of actual fear. Fearful riders should be exposed slowly to situations that cause them to feel anxiety. It would be unfair, cruel, and even dangerous to go immediately to the activity that most intimidates a fearful rider. Instead, it is important to lead up to the most fear-inducing activity by creating positive memories that can override fearful experiences. In time, the rider's brain will naturally begin to change from a fear response to one of confidence. He or she will be prepared to take the next step. Remember, however, that it takes many, many positive memories to overcome ingrained, fearful memories.

So let's begin creating positive memories.

Part 1

The Basics:
Fear and Fear-free Riding

One

Fear and the Rider's Brain

Photo by Laura Daley.

Many fearful riders mistakenly believe that their fear signals mental weakness, a failure in their riding ability, or even a deficiency in their character. After all, other people can easily do things that they cannot even imagine attempting without experiencing anxiety. They feel that they ought to be able to control their emotions and get the job done or that if they ride more, the fear will disappear.

In addition, observers often think that a fearful rider must not be a good horseperson or must need more equestrian education. People often say that fear comes from a lack of knowledge, and if that is always the case, a competent rider has no reason to be afraid. People from all parts of the horse world—from professional trainers, teachers, and riders to backyard horsemen, horse owners, and even non-horse owners—view fearful riders as less knowledgeable or less capable than riders with no confidence issues. Fearful riders may even see themselves this way. But it is not always true.

In fact, the opposite is often the case. To combat their fear, fearful riders have probably studied harder and worked more to learn riding and training skills than their confident counterparts. Because they have worked so hard to compensate for their fear issues, they have gained at least as much—if not more—knowledge and skill than the average rider.

So what holds them back? *Their emotions and their core beliefs about their true abilities* often keep such riders from progressing.

> Learning to ride fear free will bring a measure of peace not only to your riding time but to your entire life as well.

Truly letting go of fear involves more than knowledge and skill, and it is more than just gritting teeth, ignoring feelings, and performing a task. To become fear free, riders must learn to manage their emotions, understand their real strengths and weaknesses, and see what is truly happening around them. The following chapters offer specific techniques for extinguishing fear, but before addressing how to become a fear-free rider, it is important to understand fear and how it works from a scientific perspective.

Fear vs. Anxiety

If you become fearful after falling from your horse, then why are you scared when saddling up? Shouldn't you only be afraid while riding?

Have you ever been to a scary movie? You probably had a great time in the theater, but on the way through the parking lot, you might have felt nervous, and maybe for the next few days, your own dark driveway seemed a little scary too. Why? The movie alerted your subconscious to danger, and your brain began to point out every possible threat to try to keep you safe. In the same way, after a fear-inducing fall or accident, you may experience anxiety while doing everyday tasks with your horse.

Psychologists often differentiate between fear and anxiety. They define fear as an emotion that arises from an external stimulus and leads to some type of action, usually flight. Anxiety, however, arises out of unresolved fear. For example, your horse becomes unruly on a trail ride, and you experience fear as your body prepares to take action to address the situation. You try to bring the horse back under control, but the horse is too fearful and spooks sideways, unseating you. After the ride, you continue to think about the situation, causing apprehension and tension even though the scary stimulus—the out-of-control horse—is no longer present. Even though there is no external threat, you still anticipate danger. Thus, fear becomes anxiety (Öhman, 512). Fear happens in the moment, but anxiety lingers.

Although there are differences in fear and anxiety, they result in the same physical and psychological symptoms. *Riding Fear Free* deals with horse-related anxiety *and* fear, and for convenience, the terms are used interchangeably.

The Scientific Nature of Fear

Fear is more than an emotion. It is a biological survival instinct. Science backs up John Lyons when he says that "fear is common sense in disguise" (*Fear in the Rider*). Fear is an unconscious process that begins in the brain and spreads to the rest of the body. It tells people when they are in danger and starts a chain reaction that prepares them physically to keep themselves safe. When exposed to a scary situation or object, the brain prepares people either to fight or to flee.

Because it helps the body prepare to take decisive action to keep itself safe, fear can actually be a friend. Heart rate and blood pressure increase, the lungs take in more oxygen, pupils dilate to let in more light, muscles tense, and even digestion shuts down in order to save energy to face the threat. In short, the entire body becomes more alert and ready to take action. Fear can make a person stronger, faster, and more prepared to tackle a dangerous situation. In this case, fear can be an ally.

But fear can also be a foe. Reactions to even the least threatening circumstances can become overblown, causing people to feel anxiety disproportionate to what is actually happening. And in truly threatening situations, anxiety can cause a person to shut down and freeze. As a whole, fear can prevent people from leading a full and happy life, and it can keep riders from the horses they love. In this case, fear is detrimental instead of helpful. Understanding how fear works will help riders learn how to deal with it effectively.

> Fear is more than an emotion. It is a biological survival instinct. This unconscious process begins in the brain and spreads to the rest of the body to help keep you safe.

Many different sections of the brain take part in the fear reaction: the thalamus, sensory cortex, hippocampus, amygdala, and hypothalamus. The thalamus takes in information from the eyes, ears, nose, mouth, and skin and relays it to the sensory cortex, which interprets the

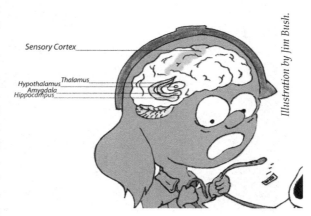

Sensory Cortex
Hypothalamus
Thalamus
Amygdala
Hippocampus

Illustration by Jim Bush.

data. The hippocampus stores and retrieves conscious memories, and it calls upon those memories to establish a context for the scary stimulus. The amygdala processes and remembers emotional responses and fear memories and sends impulses to the hypothalamus to activate fight or flight.(Layton, "How Fear Works," and Horstman, *Day in the Life of Your Brain*, 4-5).

Much of the brain's response to a fearful stimulus is unconscious and involuntary. But scientists have identified the part of the brain—the rostral cingulate—that acts as an "emotional control circuit" and actually dampens the activity of the amygdala, where fear memories are stored. Once a person consciously perceives a threat, the rostral cingulate helps to decide whether or not it is real and if action is required. In other words, it is responsible for moderating the emotional response of the brain, allowing people to achieve emotional control (Smith, "Emotional Control Circuit"). People can control their fear.

Fearful Rider/Perceptive Rider

Fearful riders are often more perceptive than others in the horse community. They are able to see the small ear twitch, feel the tensing of the horse's back muscles, or sense the tail flicks that precede a spook, bolt, or buck. Many fearful riders are actually horse-reading savants who have likely never been surprised by a horse's behavior. After an accident, they are the people who stand up, dust themselves off, and say, "I saw what was about to happen, but I didn't know how to stop it." And that is one of the key problems experienced by fearful riders: they see the minute signs of what is about to happen, but they either do not know what to do or are too frozen to take action.

The acute perception of a fearful rider will allow them to spot danger, such as this lurking cow, miles ahead of their companions.

Photo by Laura Daley.

The idea that fearful riders are highly perceptive individuals is consistent with scientific research. Scientists have discovered that anxious people are more apt to pick up unconsciously on small threat cues in their environments that people not prone to anxiety usually overlook. In addition, anxious people naturally tend to expect negative consequences when exposed to these threat cues, so their anxiety increases (Öhman, 525). Psychologists suggest that anxious people pick up details in their environments that average people do not notice (Columbia University Medical Center Newsroom, "Fleeting Images"). While most people believe the axiom that knowledge is power, in this case, knowledge in the form of increased awareness of threats can actually result in fear.

It is probably surprising to find that fearful riders are often more perceptive than their non-fearful counterparts. After all, it is desirable to be a perceptive rider and to be able to read a horse's body language or to see danger on the trail ahead. In fact, trainers, writers, and riding instructors often address the subject of equine body language and riding safety. They know that to be truly confident, a rider must accurately perceive what is happening and decide what to do in response. Acute perception is a positive trait that one expects in confident riders.

Fearful riders should be thankful for their increased ability to perceive threats, but they must learn to use their gift to spur conscious thought about what is actually happening and how to respond to the situation. One of the keys to being a fear-free rider is learning to use acute perception to lead to positive action rather than panic.

Rating Your Fear

Fear is common sense in disguise, and your feelings of fear can keep you safe, but sometimes your feelings grow out of proportion to your circumstances. In the latter case, fear is lying to you. How do you tell the difference between fear that keeps you safe and fear that tells you lies?

One method is to learn to recognize and rate your fear level. Because you cannot change something you do not realize you are doing, be honest with yourself and get in touch with your anxieties and fears. Before you can be truly fear free, you must learn to recognize, evaluate, and let go of every level of fear. There are five basic levels of horseback riding fear: *broken confidence, functioning fear, non-functioning fear, repressed fear,* and *irrational fear.*

Levels of Riding Fear

Level 1: Broken Confidence

Symptoms: This level of fear is usually found in already confident riders who have recently experienced a horse-related accident or injury. Their anxiety is often specific to the activity involved in the accident and results in nervousness about returning to that one activity rather than in a general fear of riding.

Case Study: Allison had worked with horses her whole life and was a confident, competent rider. She trained horses for clients, showed them, and even gave riding lessons. One day, she decided to ride her reliable horse bareback down her driveway to the mailbox, something she had done many times in the past. But this time, the horse stumbled and fell to his knees. Allison was able to keep her seat as the horse lunged back to his feet, but in that moment, she realized what might have happened; the accident could have been much worse, and her children could have found her lying in the driveway. The next day she purchased a riding helmet and vowed never again to ride alone, but despite her practical steps to correct the problem, her confidence had been injured. Even though she continued to train horses, for years she was unable to ride bareback, and even though her children have grown up and left home, she still hesitates to ride to her mailbox.

Level 2: Functioning Fear

Symptoms: This level of acknowledged fear does not prevent riders from working with or riding their horses. Riders are aware of the existence of fear, but they view it as an unpleasant fact and decide to live with it. They may feel anxiety when thinking about working or riding their horses, and while in the saddle, they often feel fear that is out of proportion with their circumstances, but they are able to push through and ride anyway. However, these riders are reluctant to leave their comfort zones by riding other peoples' horses or letting others ride theirs, trying new horse activities, or even doing things they used to enjoy. They may wonder why they have lost their love of adventure or reminisce about the days when they could ride fearlessly.

Case Study: Janice used to gallop across an open field, but she lost her carefree spirit. Though she continued to ride often, she grew nervous when she was around her horse and even when she thought about him. As a result, she spent most of her non-riding time complaining about her horse, the bad riding weather, the other boarders at her barn, and the behavior of the other horses. She simply did not enjoy horses and barn life the way she had in the past. Her memories of the carefree and fearless rides in childhood kept the love of horses kindled in her heart. She wanted to ride like that again, but she did not know how.

Level 3: Non-functioning Fear

Symptoms: This level of fear is so debilitating that riders may not be able to move, act, think, or even breathe when they encounter situations involving horses. They are completely unable to ride or work their animals, and they may even be unable to approach a horse or think about one without feeling a high level of anxiety.

Case Study: Sarah grew up around horses, and though she was not an avid horse lover, she was capable of handling and riding them. Over time, however, Sarah began to feel anxiety whenever she saw, heard, or even smelled a horse nearby, though she could not say exactly when or why her fear had started. She could not identify even one traumatic horse-related event that caused her to feel such terror. But later, as an adult who married and had children, Sarah simply avoided horses altogether until her daughter began to ask for riding lessons. Even though she consented to the lessons, Sarah was unable to watch her daughter in the arena or cheer her on at shows because she could not be anywhere near horses without shaking from head to toe.

Level 4: Repressed Fear

Symptoms: This level of fear exists subconsciously, so riders may feel that something is out of balance, but they are unable to identify fear as the root cause. The symptoms of repressed fear can manifest themselves in either of two extremes: timidity or overzealousness.

Timidity: Riders with repressed fear issues may have changed their riding habits, become increasingly disinterested in going to the barn, or found excuses not to spend time with horses because it is not as enjoyable at it used to be. They may be reluctant to leave their riding comfort zones and can be jealous of other people's abilities to ride or handle their horses. They feel guilty for expecting their horses to be respectful and often make excuses for why they cannot do something or why their horses behaved badly. Riders with repressed fear may try to micromanage their horses or find fault with their riding, their mount, or even their riding companions. Riders who experience this fear level have ceased to enjoy their horses, and they cannot explain why.

Case Study: On the first of the month, Sherri knew her husband would complain again about her horse's boarding bill and expenses. Their last argument had ended with her husband saying that she did nothing but complain about her horse and that she never seemed to ride. Sherri had been angry at her husband's words, but she knew that he might be right. She *had* stopped enjoying her horse, but she did not know why. Had she stopped loving horses? No. She still loved watching them on TV and shopping at tack stores. But why wasn't she more excited about spending a day at the barn with her horse, and why did every ride feel like so much work? Was it time to sell her horse?

Overzealousness: Not all riders with repressed fear react the same way. Rather than changing their behavior so that they take fewer risks, some people may actually become more aggressive in their riding habits. They may sense that something is wrong, but they do not identify fear as the root cause, and to compensate for the feelings of unease, they may grow overzealous, over-reactionary, or overconfident with their horses. They may even become reckless, taking wild risks or riding despite obviously unsafe circumstances. These types of riders may become angry at the slightest criticism and defend their horse's poor behavior while making no effort to correct it.

Case Study: Two people had to hold the horse just to get him groomed and saddled, and before teenager Dylan could even mount, his father Jim had to ride the bucks out of the horse first. Clearly, both Jim and Dylan knew their horse was unsafe, but when offered help, they felt insulted, insisted the horse was just a little nervous, and then proceeded to list all the prizes they had won in gymkhana. Despite their protests to the contrary, the horse remained out of control, and his owners were always stressed out and defensive. Jim, Dylan, and their mount persisted in attending local horse events, though they were often asked to leave in order to preserve the safety of other riders. Still, Jim and Dylan continued to ride the horse, ignoring every indication of danger by acting as if nothing were wrong. They believed they were confident and in control, but in reality, they were just along for the ride. Jim and Dylan were right to be afraid of their horse, but instead of taking steps to help the horse and themselves, they compensated for their fear by ignoring it, acting overly confident, and suffering the consequences, including injuries.

Riders may display repressed fear by decreasing their interactions with their horses or by taking too many risks with them. Any feeling of imbalance in the rider should be examined closely because hidden fear may be the cause.

Level 5: Irrational Fear

Symptoms: Irrational fear exists if riders have done all the hard mental, emotional, and physical work to extinguish fear, but they still feel afraid. Or it can manifest itself in small fears that have grown to an absurd level, and no amount of logic or emotional control seems to stop the anxiety. Riders can be in safe places, on safe horses, and doing safe activities, but their fear persists.

Case Study: Sue was deathly afraid of bees, and she refused to trail ride for that reason. She would not even get her horse out of his stall if she heard or saw a bee on the way to the barn. When a neighbor planted flowers along the fence at her boarding facility, Sue had to relocate to a barn with an indoor arena and no blooming flowers that might attract bees. She stopped accepting horseback riding invitations from friends and refrained from showing because bees might be present. Even while riding in an enclosed arena at her new flower-free boarding barn, she had to stop riding for the day if she heard flies buzzing because she imagined they were bees instead.

The exercises in this book work on both conscious and unconscious levels. As the rider consciously builds positive memories, the fear memories stored in the amygdala, which unconsciously influence the fear response, are overridden and the body's response to fear becomes less aggressive. As the rider learns to ask good questions about a certain situation and respond appropriately, he or she strengthens the conscious moderating response that takes place in the rostral cingulate. On both conscious and subconscious levels, the rider is working to extinguish fear.

Beginning the Journey

The journey to riding fear free is personal, and it requires hard work. This is no movie montage in which the world is made right during the course of a song and some video clips. You should celebrate the grit and determination you as an individual will use in overcoming your riding fears, but it is also important to build a good support system. Find a good mentor, friend, or teacher to help you along the way, or visit RidingFearFree.com to find supporters online.

Now, let's see how it works.

Notes

Two

Fear Extinction and Conditioned Response

Photo by Jim Bush.

People can train their brains to override fearful memories with positive memories. *Fear extinction* is the scientific name for this conditioned-response method of countering the brain's fear response (Layton, "How Fear Works," and Tamminga, "The Anatomy of Fear Extinction"). In other words, fear extinction is a way of creating positive memories to replace and override the fearful memories stored in the brain. As a result of replacing fearful memories, riders will begin to feel less anxious while with their horses—or even just thinking about their horses—and their response to fearful stimuli will become proportionate to their actual circumstances.

Conditioned response is a learned reaction to a stimulus. Trainers often use conditioned-response methods in their work with horses. For example, they teach the horse to turn to the right by picking up the right rein, holding it until the horse turns, and then releasing it. The horse learns that pressure on the right rein means the rider is asking him to turn right, and his reward is the release of the pressure on his mouth. This action is repeated until the horse learns to respond consistently to the stimulus of the right rein by turning to the right.

Even though humans are more emotionally complex than horses, conditioned response also works in dealing with people. Fearful riders have to learn a new response to stimuli that might

> Fearful riders often look back and wonder what happened to those carefree days in the saddle. You can experience them again, and your memories of the good times will help. So keep looking back.

have originally caused them to freeze or panic. They must experience a dose of the scary object or circumstance small enough that they feel no anxiety and are able to practice the desired (fear-free) response. This creates a good memory of the object or circumstance. As a result of many fear-free repetitions, the brain will begin to change from reacting with a fearful response to reacting based on new, good memories. In the same way that the horse is taught to turn to the right by using pressure and release of pressure on the right rein, so are humans taught to create new, positive memories through a natural progression of pressure and release or approach and retreat.

Replacing Fear Memories with Positive Memories

Replacing and overriding a single fear memory requires many good memories. That sounds like a daunting task. If so many good memories are necessary to overcome just one fearful one, then it may sound as if you'll be in the saddle for years before you make any improvements. But that's not necessarily the case. Very few hours in the saddle are required to become fear free as long as you are willing to use the techniques for building many fear-free memories in a short amount of time. Overcoming fear does take time, however, and while there are ways to streamline the process, the primary concern is quality and thoroughness rather than speed.

So how exactly does one create positive new memories?

Traditionally, riding instructors, trainers, and even the fearful riders themselves start their journey by going straight to the fearful activity—or close to it—and trying to practice it until the fear disappears. It seems logical. For example, the rider is afraid of jumping. She has fear memories centered on jumping, or she deals with many theoretical fears or "what-if" questions. What if the horse balks? What if I fall off? It seems to make sense that the only way to build good memories of jumping is to jump.

That is certainly true. But it is not the first step in the journey. It is the last step. Why? Because the goal is not merely to jump. The goal is to jump fear free, and the only way to accomplish this is by first creating positive memories to override the fearful ones. If you begin by setting up a jump and forcing yourself to ride it repeatedly, you are actually accomplishing the opposite of what you wish to do. Instead of creating fear-free memories of jumping, you are further ingraining your fear memories by continuing to jump even though you still feel afraid.

Instead, you must begin where you experience no fear. It sounds counterintuitive, but it is nonetheless true. *In order to be effective, positive memories do not have to replicate the exact fearful circumstances.* You can compile any good horse-related memories to override the brain's learned response to fear. Situations do not necessarily have to correspond precisely to the fearful memory, but they can gradually build up to the frightening activity.

First, you must begin where you feel safe and at ease and gradually expand your comfort zones without pushing so far that you become anxious. Second, you must understand the value of the repetition of short rides. It takes hundreds and thousands of rides to overcome fearful memories, but that doesn't mean you have to spend five hours in the saddle each day. Lots of short rides are more valuable in overcoming fear than one long ride.

Becoming Fear Free
through Pressure and Release / Approach and Retreat

What do you do when a horse is afraid? How do you teach a horse to do something like trailer loading, which looks perfectly safe to you but seems like a dangerous situation to the horse? Horses are already naturally fearful of enclosed spaces because, as prey animals they have the instinct to run when they sense danger. An enclosed space takes away their one method of sure safety. Add to the equation that the contraption you're asking them to enter feels unstable, echoes with every footstep, and actually flies down the road at 55 miles per hour. To a horse, this looks like certain death! He has every reason to be afraid.

How do you begin to teach a horse to get inside a trailer without being terrified? Do you simply walk up to the trailer and expect him to get over it and step right in? Do you drag him in? Do you set up a winch and pull him in? You can. You will have the horse in the trailer, but have you actually done anything to make the horse feel calm during the trip? Have you addressed the fear, or have you just dealt with his physical circumstances?

Of course you wouldn't force the horse into the trailer. In the long run, you know it is better to teach him that it is perfectly safe, even though it seems to go against his natural instincts. Most people use approach and retreat/pressure and release to work the horse's emotions until he willingly loads on his own. You would gradually bring the horse closer to the trailer and take him away to a "safe spot." Then you would go a step closer and retreat again. Eventually, you would ask for one foot to touch the trailer and retreat. Then two feet and retreat. Then three feet and retreat. Then the whole horse and retreat. By taking it one foot at a time and retreating in between, you show the horse that you don't want everything from him now, but he is safe to take the next step without worrying that he's immediately going to become trapped: his biggest fear.

You work the horse's emotions in a low-stress, methodical way and show him that he is safe. By adding pressure and taking it away, you prove that you will never ask of him more than he is capable of giving. You are growing his confidence with each new step of the process and creating good memories of the trailer with each approach. You are dealing with the whole horse: the mind and the body.

Photo by Laura Daley.

Trainers prepare a horse's body, mind, and spirit so that he is willing to load himself into the trailer, a contraption that takes away his ability to flee—his biggest fear ever. Why not be as kind to yourself by preparing your body, mind, and spirit before trying to face your fears?

The journey does not end there. Once the horse loads safely at home, you would not immediately put him in the trailer, haul for three hours on a windy road, ride all day, and then expect him to reload happily. Instead, you would start with short trips around the block, driving slowly and carefully. Then you would gradually build up to rides to town, hauling the horse to the grocery store and back. You would build on the horse's trailer experience using fun, safe, easy trips to create positive, fear-free memories in his mind.

Next, when the horse loads and unloads consistently, you would take him on short trips to other places, like a trail ride or schooling show. You would expose him briefly to the excitement of a new place, possibly riding or walking him around, and then return home to a good rub down or extra bite of food.

Finally, when the horse tells you that the trailer is no longer an issue, you can take that windy trip to ride the Sierras all day and expect him to load willingly afterward. But even then, if he hesitates at any stage of this process, you would simply take a step back to do a quick review of what he learned at home and tap into his conditioned response. Eventually, you would have him trailer loading in the most difficult situation imaginable, including major storms, barn fires, and crazy horses milling around.

But fearful riders (and their teachers) are often not as kind to themselves as they are to their horses. They may take every tiny step necessary to trailer load a horse so that they address his fear, but when it comes to their own fear, they expect to be able to get over it and walk right into the trailer, so to speak. And even once they begin getting over their fears, they expect to be able to tackle a 100-mile endurance race or take that dream cattle-drive vacation right away.

Why?

Why would you slowly and methodically tame your horse's fear and then force yourself straight into the very activity that terrifies you? Why rush yourself through the process? Why not be as kind to yourself as you are to your horse? Why not address your whole self—body, mind, and spirit—so that in the long run, you will be in a far better place?

Pressure and release (or approach and retreat) forms one of the foundations of *Riding Fear Free*. By raising your anxiety level without actually making yourself fearful and then taking away the scary stimulus, you create fear-free memories, learn to see reality, and retrain your brain to handle a real emergency.

Disrupting Fear Memories

Researchers have discovered that extinction therapy is most effective during a phase known as "memory reconsolidation," when a person is actively retrieving, or recalling, a memory (Society for Neuroscience, "Fear and PTSD"). During reconsolidation, the memory can either be reinforced or altered (Suzuki et al., "Memory Reconsolidation"). In fact, different chemical processes take place depending on whether the memory is reinforced or altered. The brain literally changes.

Therefore, one of the most effective techniques for loosening the grip of fear memories on the brain, especially if one particular circumstance triggered the rider's anxiety, is to recall the traumatic event while actually remaining safe and unharmed and to envision a better outcome. By recalling the scary event and deliberately changing the ending, people can weaken and disrupt the brain's fear memories and replace them with a new, equally valid positive version of the event.

There is a proper time for riders to attempt recalling their traumatic memories, however, and it only comes *after* they have built many fear-free memories and learned the proper techniques for controlling their emotions. There is also a proper place to begin altering fear memories, and that is *away* from your horse. Riders will begin this process in the safety of their homes and only attempt it with their horses or under saddle if they are truly comfortable.

Fearless vs. Fear-free

This book is not designed to teach riders to be *fearless*. Because fear is the body's mechanism for keeping itself safe, being fearless means that the body is no longer able to detect and prepare for danger. Fearless riders either ignore or fail to see the hazards before them. They disregard the signals their horses send them, and this can, and often does, end in an avoidable accident. This makes fearless riders dangerous.

In contrast, *fear-free* riding is not riding *without fear*. It is actually learning to think through fear, decide what to do, and then act accordingly. Fear-free riding taps into your God-given ability to detect danger and your capability to use your conscious mind to decide how best to respond. As you learn to think through your initial feelings of fear, you will build new, positive memories to cancel out your fearful memories, thus leveling out your fear response so that it is proportional to what is actually happening.

Fear-free riders are both free from paralyzing fear *and* free to use their instincts to perceive the real dangers before them and act accordingly. One of the main issues that anxious riders face is that their fear response is out of proportion to the fearful stimulus, and learning to overcome this is one of the critical factors in riding fear free. To achieve the state of being fear free, riders must begin to extinguish their fear by building positive memories.

But how?

It often seems as if no one really has the answer for helping you overcome your fears. Even the advice of the most well-meaning friend, trainer, or instructor may feel as if it is missing a step.

> **Step 1:** Get on horse, feel afraid, but keep riding.
> **Step 2:** ?
> **Step 3:** Ride without fear.

What is step 2?

Step 2 is to address your thoughts and feelings as you are exposed to small, manageable doses of a fear-inducing stimulus and then released from that pressure. This process leads to riding fear free.

Three

Common Advice for Fearful Riders

Photo by Laura Daley

Fearful riders often seek the help of trusted, horse-knowledgeable friends and teachers and search for advice in books and magazines, and most of these sources provide valuable pieces of the fear-free puzzle. The techniques and advice listed in this chapter can provide a good foundation for becoming fear free, and in some cases, they alone may be enough to help certain riders regain confidence. But to become truly fear free, most riders need more.

It is important to remember that the goal is not just to canter in a field, jump a fence, or ride in a show. The goal is to do these things fear free. Every ride either reinforces fear or weakens it in your brain, so when you ride *despite* fear, you are actually making your fear memories *stronger*, which is the opposite of the desired result. And unfortunately, most of the common advice given to fearful riders encourages them to continue the activities regardless of their fear.

Few people in the horse industry specialize in helping fearful riders, which is unfortunate since most equine professionals have probably encountered them in their years on the job. Most of the time, when fearful riders seek help, they find it in the form of either horse trainers or riding instructors, and this is not necessarily bad. Both types of specialists have access to the tools they need in order to help. They already understand that they cannot begin with the goal; they have to work up to it. No riding instructor would put a

> Fearful riders have already heard all the common advice—from buying a more secure saddle to taking riding lessons—but those are just physical changes. The rider's mind has been neglected.

beginning rider on a horse and start teaching canter pirouettes right away. First, she would teach the basics—walk, trot, canter, balance, rein control—and when the rider was ready, she would teach the canter pirouette. And no horse trainer would get on an unstarted horse without teaching him the basic cues—give to pressure, stop, turn—from the ground first. The trainer would take each step to ensure that the horse was ready to accept a rider. This is exactly what should be done with a fearful rider's emotions. Trainers and instructors already understand the general concept, but they fail to apply it to riders' emotions.

When faced with a fearful rider, a trainer usually seeks a horse-training solution: if we can just get the horse's body under control, then the rider will gain confidence. The riding instructor finds a riding-technique solution: if we can just get the rider balanced, he will feel less unstable and therefore more confident.

Those are physical aspects of riding fear free, but the most important parts of the equation – the mind and spirit of the rider – are viewed as by-products of perfecting the other tasks. In actuality, the emotions of the fearful rider ought to be the main concern. And because trainers and instructors already understand that small steps are needed to reach the end goal, they have the basic understanding of what they need to do to help a fearful rider.

Below are some common—and not entirely bad—pieces of advice that fearful riders may encounter from well-meaning professionals. Most of the advice falls into two categories:

> ### Two Categories of
> ### Common Advice for Fearful Riders
> (1) Improve something physical, and the rider will become more confident.
>
> (2) Ignore fear and push through anyway, and the rider will gain confidence.

As we examine some of this advice, it will become clear that the rider's brain—the most important aspect of the process—is ignored.

RIDING FEAR FREE 21

Confidence through Physical Improvement

Take Riding Lessons. The first suggestion fearful riders often hear is to take riding lessons, and with good reason. Lessons on a reliable horse with a good instructor can be a huge help. They can help improve balance and overall technique, and they can help to create the good memories that are needed to replace fearful ones.

But it is vitally important to find the right instructor. Fearful riders need teachers who understand their issues and who are willing to take the lessons slowly, gradually building confidence until the students can attain each small goal without being pushed. They must not press their students to the next step. If a rider needs to be pushed in order to take a particular step, then he or she is not ready for it yet. A teacher's goal should be to leave the student always wanting more.

Unfortunately, it is difficult to find teachers who truly understand how to help, so it is important for you to be candid about your fear issues and make it clear that you want to go slow. If you feel pushed, it is important to go back to a comfortable lesson and let the new skill evolve naturally.

Get in Shape. Often, after being told to take lessons, a fearful rider is advised to get in shape physically: lose weight, build muscle, develop endurance, become more flexible. No doubt this is good advice, not only for riding fear free but for quality of life and general health.

This is especially good advice for fearful riders. Although you may not realize it, a physical issue may actually hinder your confidence. For example, overly tight inner thigh tendons may prevent you from sitting correctly in the saddle, resulting not only in chronic pain but in a less secure position. It is not necessary to become a specimen of physical perfection to ride without fear, but it is important to examine physical strengths and weaknesses and to make changes that will help keep you safe, develop more confidence, and eliminate pain.

But getting in shape will not magically make you fear free because body condition is not the underlying problem; the problem is fear. While losing weight and exercising may make the journey easier, it will not eliminate all physical issues. Every person has her own physical limitations, including weight problems, allergies, and other physical disabilities. No one should let physical issues stop him from taking the journey to fear-free riding.

Change Tack. Again, this advice can be helpful to a fearful rider. If your tack is unsafe, worn out, or causing pain to either horse or rider, it is important to make a change if possible. Tack can consciously or unconsciously put up a roadblock on the path to riding fear free, and it is often one of the simplest fixes. Amid your other fears, you should not have to worry about whether or not the saddle will slip, and you should not expect your horse to perform perfectly in an ill-fitting, pain-inducing saddle. Experiment with tack. Find out what reins feel best, what saddle feels the most secure, or what stirrups ease ankle pain. Removing doubts and ending pain from poorly fitted tack will smooth the fear-free journey. Changing tack will not result in an instant fix, but it can clear another stumbling block from the path to fear-free riding.

Too much focus on tack can actually become a diversion from the real problem: fear. It is easy to get stuck in the search for the perfect saddle or to use tack as an excuse to delay the journey to riding fear free. Even though having the perfect saddle can help, it is not absolutely necessary. If you can't afford new equipment, you can still work toward becoming fear free by adjusting your lessons to your individual needs. For example, you may have to ride only five or ten minutes at a time. And it costs nothing to dream of the possibilities and remember fun, easy rides. Having the best of everything will not create a better horseperson or a more confident rider. Some of the best moments between a horse and rider cost nothing more than the willingness to be silent, open your heart, close your mouth, and enjoy the moment.

Also, the suggestion to reevaluate a horse's tack does not include the idea of getting bigger, more powerful saddles/bits/tie downs/spurs/whips as a substitute for good training. While you may need to change or replace these items, you should not do so with the intention of forcing the horse into submission or to artificially feel more secure. Training is the best—and only—way to ensure that the horse will respond to the rider's requests as he or she is on the journey to riding fear free.

Train the Horse to Develop Trust. Most resources designed to help fearful riders focus on training the horse, and this is not wrong. Having a well-trained equine partner is an important part of becoming fear free. Before you can trust your mount, you must see that the horse will respond to your cues. The horse must stop when you say stop. He must go when you say go. He must maintain the speed you set. He must turn when you touch the rein. And he must do these things willingly on the first request. Seeking the help of a professional trainer is often a good idea.

So training the horse is important, but to become truly fear free, the rider also needs training. If you have sought help from a professional, you must learn what the horse has been taught. It does no good to send a horse away for thirty days and have him trained to do any task perfectly if you do not know how to ask the horse to do that task when he returns home. You must learn how the horse is trained, and you must learn the cues to elicit the same responses.

More important, you must also be trained mentally and emotionally; you must learn to become fear free. The goal is to ride fear free, not to maneuver a perfectly trained horse while you are still afraid. The only way to become fear free is to acknowledge fear, process it, and release it by creating new, positive memories to replace the old fear memories.

"Confidence" through Repressing Fear

Just Calm Down. Everyone strives for calm. The market is full of self-help books and yoga videos designed to help people relax and deal with their stressful lives. It is easy to let circumstances and busy lives become overwhelming and cause anxiety, but it takes work to relax in stressful or fear-inducing circumstances. For an already fearful rider, it can be even more difficult.

The ultimate goal for every encounter between an equine and a human should be that both the horse and the rider are calmer after their time together. But how do you achieve such calm? It takes more than being told to "calm down." It takes the willingness to start where you are already calm, even if that means just standing beside the horse and brushing him or sitting at a desk, writing down your goals, and allowing yourself to progress naturally by using the tools described in the later chapters of this book.

Breathe. "Don't forget to breathe!" That phrase is heard often in exercise videos and in lesson rings around the world. When exerting physical effort or experiencing a stressful situation, people often hold their breath without realizing it. Obviously, this is not a good thing.

Holding your breath not only causes dizziness or fainting but also creates tension in your body that translates to the horse. If you are holding your breath and feeling tense, then the horse may also begin to feel anxious. This starts a downward spiral for a fearful rider. The rider makes the horse tense, and in turn, the horse makes the rider tenser. By breathing properly, a rider can avoid this situation.

One of the best ways to remember to breathe—other than simply having someone tell you to do so—is to sing. Sing anything: top-40 hits, hymns, or even the ABC's. Singing encourages *correct breathing*. A nervous person takes shallow breaths, using only the chest muscles. But proper breathing comes from the diaphragm. The belly should expand with each inhale and contract with each exhale. Correct breathing helps release tension and prevents it from affecting the horse. Singing will help correct breathing occur more naturally.

> Every ride either strengthens or weakens fear memories in your brain. So any time you ride despite your fear, you are actually reinforcing fear's hold on you. To overcome it once and for all, you must begin where you feel *no* fear.

Cowboy Up and Just Do It. Riders, both English and western, descend from a proud heritage and legacy of great horsepeople, and there are many traditions to follow. As a result, horses have been ridden and trained in basically the same manner for hundreds, if not thousands, of years. These horsepeople are quoted and revered even today.

Fearful riders and their teachers often believe that the right way to handle fear is to get tough like John Wayne, who said, "Courage is being scared to death but saddling up anyway." Although it is difficult to argue with such an icon, that is not courage. If fear is common sense in disguise, then taking an action in spite of that fear is insanity. Those who don't listen to their fear are often injured in a dangerous situation.

True courage is not gritting one's teeth through a scary situation. True courage is accepting that fear exists, working through it, releasing it, and then tackling the situation unencumbered.

Many in the western riding tradition proudly proclaim that riders ought to "cowboy up." This phrase makes a great bumper sticker, but for the fearful rider, it is a major roadblock to becoming fear free.

Fake It 'til You Make It. Closely related to "just do it" and "cowboy/cowgirl up," this piece of advice translates into a bad idea: hide your fear. Pretend it isn't there. Don't acknowledge it. Ignore it. Act as if you're confident, and eventually you will be.

Like most pieces of advice fearful riders hear, this does have a basis in reality. Horses sense body language and respond accordingly. A nervous-looking handler results in an unsure, nervous horse. So it is good to project confidence as much as possible. Walk tall, with your chest out and with purposeful strides, but don't try to walk away from fear.

Faking it can help you accomplish a riding goal, and it may seem like it helps you develop confidence. But the fear does not go away. It only latches more strongly and hides deeper. The only way to become truly fear free is to acknowledge fear, process it, and release it. The same is true for every powerful emotion—anger, shame, grief—that seems to control your life.

Decide to Change and Then Change. Also related to "just do it," this practical suggestion is often incredibly frustrating for a fearful rider who wants nothing more than to stop being afraid and to accomplish riding goals. But this piece of advice suggests that a decision to change will result in *instant* change—that you can simply decide to become fear free and then make it happen through sheer force of will. This is simply not true. The brain must be taught to react differently to the activities that cause fear. That takes time.

The road to becoming fear free does begin with the willingness—with the decision—to change. But that is step one, and complete change is *not* step two. It is much further down the line. Fearful riders must learn how to change. They must practice the techniques for changing. Those techniques must become part of their subconscious. Only then is change achieved.

Find a Job to Do. Fearful riders are often accused of over-thinking the issue and are told to do a job as a way of shifting their focus from something negative (fear) to something positive (job). This type of distraction from fear is not necessarily bad in the right circumstances. Before this technique can work, however, riders must be further along in the journey. They must already be able to tell when their feelings match their circumstances and when they do not. If a rider feels afraid when the situation is actually safe, then being distracted by a small, attainable job or goal is one option among many for dealing with fear.

This does not mean that it is advisable to tackle a big job or that it is good to use this distraction technique as the only tool to combat fear. Taking on a large-scale job, such as going on a cattle drive or volunteering on a search-and-rescue team, is actually a good way to ensure that you will grit your teeth and do the job despite your fear, thus reinforcing it. Again, reinforcing fear is not the goal. The aim of this book is to help riders become fear free, and distraction alone is not the solution.

Changing Old Beliefs: A Comparison

Riding Fear Free presents an alternative to traditional advice. While still respecting time-tested horse-training and riding techniques, this book focuses on the real issue: fear. Many of your old beliefs about what you should and should not do—some of which are based on poor logic—will be challenged.

For example, how many times have you been told that you should not dismount when you find yourself getting nervous or are having trouble getting a horse to obey your cues?

If you're like most riders, you've probably heard this often.

But have you ever asked yourself why?

Though the origin is uncertain, there is a prominent myth in the horse world that dismounting is a sign of submission and weakness. Dismounting means you admit that your horse has beaten you. It means that you have failed in some way.

But what horse has ever learned anything through only one repetition? Besides, horse training is not a competition that pits you against your horse. On the contrary, horse training is about developing a partnership in which you and your animal work together to achieve a common goal. If your lesson isn't working out and you find that both you and the horse are becoming frustrated, sometimes the best thing you can do for your partnership is to walk away and reevaluate what is happening.

Above all, do not fall victim to the misinformation that stopping a lesson before it is completely taught will somehow ruin the horse or make it more difficult the next time you try to teach him. The horse does not know when the lesson was supposed to end, so he won't congratulate himself on the way back to the barn for "winning the battle." He's going to think that you intended to stop at that point all along.

You are never more than a few minutes away from stopping any lesson. Dismount if you need to dismount.

Let's examine some other real-life examples.

> Horse training doesn't pit you against your horse. It's the chance to develop a partnership.

Illustration by Lydia Beccard.

Riding Fear Free Says

They Say: Stay calm.

***Riding Fear Free* Says:** We agree (mostly). In general, if you stay calm, your horse will too. But horses do have their own emotions, and they are entitled to flinch if something startles them, just as you are. Furthermore, if you never get excited, then neither you nor your horse will ever practice getting excited and calming down afterward. That's why it's important to work through your emotions in a controlled environment. When a big scare comes, both you and your horse will be used to regaining control and calming down quickly.

They Say: Slow down and stop if you become emotional.

***Riding Fear Free* Says:** Sometimes slowing down is the right answer, but if you are in a controlled environment and safe surroundings, then you should consider practicing raising and lowering your emotions. Take the situation to an absurd level in your mind, but don't physically make a spook so big that you panic. Keep thinking or talking about the absurd scenario until it is so overblown and out of proportion to reality that you have to stop and take stock of the true situation. Once you stop and ask good questions about what is truly happening, you will see that reality was not as big as your fears led you to believe.

They Say: Challenge yourself.

***Riding Fear Free* Says:** Introduce a concept and let it evolve naturally. If you are challenging or pushing, then you are ignoring your fear and pushing ahead in spite of it.

They Say: Never lead a scared rider on a horse.

***Riding Fear Free* Says:** If that is where the rider feels comfortable, then lead her. Now is the time to experience the comfort and movement of the horse without the stress or worry of having to control him. This way, the rider can focus on her other senses and enjoy the experience that has caused her fear for so long.

They Say: You must have the proper brand and type of equipment.

***Riding Fear Free* Says:** You do not need the most expensive, advanced equipment to work with your horse. A simple halter and thin stick can work just as well as the most expensive halter, lead, and dressage whip.

They Say: The only emotion to bring to the barn is a sense of humor.

***Riding Fear Free* Says:** If it were always easy for you to laugh, then you would never be afraid. Give yourself permission to bring all your emotions to the barn so that you can work through them and then let them go. Once you are able to control your emotions in a healthy way, you will be able to leave them at the barn door and bring in your sense of humor. Note that, while it's okay to feel anger during the process, you should not mistreat your horse or put yourself in danger. You must find a way of safely letting your anger go. If you find you need additional help, please consult a professional.

They Say: Get back on after a fall, runaway, or scare.

Riding Fear Free **Says:** Stop and evaluate the situation. Do *not* get back on the horse unless that is where you are ready to continue in your riding journey. Though others may tell you differently, you are not teaching your horse that a fall, runaway, or scare is the way to get out of a lesson, thus encouraging more of that behavior. Horses do not like being scared, and they do not try to get out of work by spooking themselves to the point that their flight instincts kick in. By taking a step back and evaluating the situation, you are actually making sure that you are ready to continue the lesson and succeed in teaching it. You cannot teach effectively or learn if you are in a fearful state. As mentioned above, you are never more than a few minutes from stopping any lesson, and your horse will not know the difference.

Quite a few first-time riders who have fallen and gotten back on the horse actually stop riding altogether once they leave the scene of the accident. Every horse lover has heard friends say that they hate horses or are scared of them because of a frightening childhood event. Maybe a horse, pony, or mule ran away with them when they were children, and they were forced to get back on and ride before they were ready. And that was likely the last time they ever rode. Why? They were not allowed to recover emotionally from the incident and were forced to ride in a fearful state. How could that possibly be fun? Why would they ever want to ride again?

People may say that you will be *more* scared the next time you ride if you don't get back in the saddle immediately, but this is not necessarily true. A big adrenaline rush will pass over time, leaving you calmer when you greet your horse again, and you will have left behind the physical effects of the accident. Rather than dwelling on your fear or refusing to acknowledge it, if you process the accident and your feelings about it, you will actually be in a much stronger position when you choose to return to the saddle.

They Say: You don't just get over irrational fear. It's irrational. Because fear is not a conscious choice, it is impossible for a rider to change the way they naturally react to their circumstances.

Riding Fear Free **Says:** Whether or not a particular fear is rational or irrational, it's true that you don't "just get over" it. But the belief that fear cannot be overcome is simply untrue. This misapprehension allows people to avoid facing their fears. Brain science has shown that people can replace fears—rational or irrational—by making a conscious choice to retrain their brains. It is hard work, but it can be done.

They Say: You can only become a fear-free rider with lots of wet saddle blankets and hours of riding.

Riding Fear Free **Says:** Because much of the hard work involves retraining a fearful rider's way of thinking, the truth is that little actual saddle time is needed to become fear free. Because *Riding Fear Free* is about more than simply doing a physical task, the most extensive work occurs in the rider's mind. Wet tissues develop a fear-free rider faster than wet saddle blankets.

They Say: Avoid falling off the horse at all costs.

Riding Fear Free **Says:** Falling is not fun, but it is an unavoidable part of riding: what goes up must come down. So if you realize you are about to fall, make the decision to do so correctly by allowing the momentum to flow through your whole body so that you do not hit the ground at only one or two points. The best way to avoid injury in a fall is to divide the impact energy. For example, if a person jumped out a third-story window and tried to absorb all the impact at once with his feet, he would most likely break his legs. But a person can safely descend the same distance and effectively absorb the exact same amount of impact energy by using the stairs. He is still traveling or "falling" the same distance and absorbing the same overall impact, but he is breaking up the energy and absorbing it in safe increments.

In order to apply this to riding, it is necessary to divide the energy of your fall across the entire surface of your body by rolling with the momentum so that no one point is forced to endure the impact at one time. Like each step you take down the stairs, in a fall, each part of your body absorbs a little of the impact. Practice falling and rolling short distances in a controlled environment, and then build to longer distances and faster speeds. This way, in an emergency you will be less likely to brace or fight against the fall and more likely to absorb its energy safely and minimize your risk of injury.

They Say: Never let your horse eat while you are riding.

Riding Fear Free **Says:** Some state parks do not allow horses to graze, and it is rude to let your horse eat the profits from a neighbor's field. But if it is permissible where you ride, it is fine to train your horse to eat on command. Taking a two-minute snack break can help steady a nervous horse and rider. You can teach your horse a cue that tells him when it is okay to eat with a bridle on and when it is not. If you are concerned about allowing a horse to graze with the bit, leave a halter under the bridle and remove the bit for snack time. However, if you cannot be consistent, it is better to prohibit eating than to fight a horse that is snatching at grass as you ride.

They Say: The rider looks confident and rides so well; she can't possibly be afraid.

Riding Fear Free **Says:** Looks can be deceiving. Stoic or even daredevil riders can mask their fear. They may appear to be in control, but that does not mean they are in touch with their emotions or that they can handle themselves or their horses in an emergency.

Why Some Riders Need More

All the traditional advice in this chapter contains some truth, and it can take you a long way, especially if your fear falls into the broken confidence level. But the goal of this book is not to help you ride *despite* fear; it is to help you ride *fear free*. And while all of the advice in this chapter is helpful, none of it addresses specific ways to deal with the mental aspects of fear. Most of the advice involves changing something physical, not changing your thought process. Worse, many of the tips actually encourage you to ignore or circumvent fear, and some urge you to disregard or hide fear and push onward.

Every ride either reinforces fear or weakens it in your brain; therefore, riding *despite* fear makes the memories *stronger*, not weaker. So rather than ignoring fear and thus reinforcing it, it is much better to begin where you experience no fear, thus weakening your fear memories. From that point forward, every step along the path should evolve naturally out of the one before, and after every ride, you should look forward to the next, not dread it.

This is not to say that the journey is easy or that the burden of fear is light. The road to riding fear free is emotional, and walking it requires a great commitment to change, but you should never be pushed beyond—or even too close to—your physical and emotional limits. The trip to fear-free riding should always leave you wanting more.

Four

General Principles of Riding Fear Free

Photo by Laura Daley.

Before getting into the specifics of becoming fear free, it is important to know the general principles involved in the process.

No Pushing

You will never be asked to do more than you are capable of giving freely. One hard-and-fast rule of learning to ride fear free is this: if you are in a fearful state, do not get on your horse. If at any time you become fearful, stop. Completely remove yourself from the fearful situation, and then reevaluate how to proceed from there. Only do what you feel comfortable doing. If you are in an emotional state and cannot seem to change your thinking, do not get on your horse. Period.

Whether or not you are working with a teacher or trainer, the temptation to push yourself—or to allow yourself to be pushed—will always exist. Most teachers will have the best of intentions, and they desire to help you reach your goal. In fact, they will believe in you probably more than you believe in yourself. They will see your skill as a horseperson and respect your talents as a horse reader, and sometimes this will tempt them to push a bit. They know you can do it physically, even if you are still fearful about it. They're the professionals, and that's why you hired them, so it's best to trust your teacher, right?

Wrong.

> Always begin where you experience no fear, even if that means staying on the ground while your friends are riding. New fear-free memories of horses can be created anywhere: under saddle, on the ground, or even at home.

Only you can judge when it's time to move to the next step. It must be your decision alone. Why? The goal of these lessons is not to undertake an activity despite your fear but to do it *fear free*. Until you are *completely* comfortable with the early steps of your lesson plan, you should not go further. As you work through your exercises, *you* will naturally take the next step, and it will not feel like a big deal. It will feel as if it grew out of the work you have done all along.

Capturing Your Thoughts

Random thoughts pop into our brains all the time, but we do not have to act on every one. In the past, an idle thought may have become so strong in your mind that it caused you to become fearful. But you can learn to evaluate each thought and decide if it has merit, if you should store it for later, or if you should discard it. When a thought or what-if question enters your mind, you can use good questions to counter it, or you can choose to write it down to ponder later and go right back to your activity.

Some random thoughts help us become aware of danger or help us change our situation for the better, so it is unwise to dismiss thoughts even during a great riding lesson. For this reason, it is essential that you learn to capture your thoughts. Then, you can choose which ones have value and require action and which ones you elect to let go. Learning to control your thoughts, both negative and positive, will help you bring peace and stability to your emotions.

Controlling Your Emotions

Euripides said that "courage may be taught as a child is taught to speak," and that is what you will gain when you learn to control your emotions. Most truly fearful riders have already pursued the usual avenues—lessons and training—and still deal with nagging fear. The solution to the problem of fear in this case is emotional control, which you can achieve in much the same way a horse learns to control his emotions: through pressure and release. You'll move to the boundaries of your fear but not beyond. And you'll only do what you are comfortable doing. Over time, the boundaries will begin to move and change, and soon you'll start doing things that you once considered terrifying.

Asking Good Questions and Seeing Reality

Fearful riders often experience fear that is out of proportion with what is actually happening. One of the keys to riding fear free is seeing reality and reacting accordingly. By asking questions as you experience small amounts of anxiety, you'll learn to judge whether your situation is truly dangerous or if your fear is blowing the situation out of proportion in your mind.

If after asking good questions and assessing what is really happening, you judge that the situation is safe, then you will be able to change your thinking by replacing fears with facts. If you find that you are in a dangerous situation, you will experience an appropriate sense of fear that corresponds to your circumstances. Because you have practiced controlling both your thinking and your emotions in a safe environment, you are able to feel fear in proportion to what is happening. You will be less likely to freeze and more likely to make the right choices to keep yourself and your horse safe.

> Riding despite your fear only reinforces it. In order to ride fear free, you must begin where you feel no anxiety so that you can change the way your brain reacts to horses.

Celebrating Improvement

Fearful riders will learn to celebrate even the smallest accomplishment. This will not only help make riding enjoyable again but will also make every ounce of progress apparent. Celebration helps riders realize that the big goal is possible because they have seen all the steps and successes along the way.

In your lessons, you will be encouraged to start with physical actions—approach and retreat, pressure and release, ups and downs—in order to mark each new stage of your progression. These physical actions mark a stopping point and a new beginning. During each action, you should celebrate what you have already done. Eventually, you will not have to take a physical action to mark a new beginning. Instead, you will be able to acknowledge a small step, celebrate mentally, and continue doing the same actions without a physical change.

Some people will find physical celebration difficult. Most adults have learned to behave properly in public, and that means overt displays of emotion feel wrong. People who struggle with outward displays of emotion need to realize that unlocking their ability to celebrate and acknowledge success, no matter how small, improves confidence and overrides the doubts and negative thoughts that may try to sneak in after a good moment.

The ability to see and understand your progress and to give yourself a mental release is one of the keys to your success. Your chance to progress will be almost unlimited if you do not skip this step, no matter how far along you are in the process or how accomplished you become as a rider. The celebration of success can change your thinking pattern if you apply it every time you ride. Much more than a beginner maneuver, celebration of every small accomplishment is a vital change in the way you understand your actions, and it is a redefinition of pressure and success.

Processing Time

Fearful riders need time to process what they have learned in lessons. The brain cannot always deal with information thoroughly when a rider is receiving a lot of stimuli at the same time, and it needs down time to process what happened. By walking away immediately after trying something new, riders will progress along the learning curve faster than if they had drilled themselves for hours. Taking time—days or weeks—between lessons or rides actually helps the brain better prepare itself for the next time the rider attempts the new skill.

> Fearful riders usually face an imbalance in the risk/reward ratio. They are asked to take a very big risk, such as a long trail ride, and in exchange, the change in their fear level is very small. Usually, they are simply pleased they survived.

Photo by Laura Daley.

How?

Small risks and rewards will add up to big benefits. When fearful riders choose to try to overcome fear using traditional wisdom, they usually face an imbalance in the risk/reward ratio. They are asked to take a very big risk (or what they perceive to be a very big risk), and in exchange, their actual return (the change in their fear level) is small. For example, if a teacher encourages you to tackle a big fear head-on, like going on a three-hour trail ride, that is a big risk to you. You will be anxious for three hours, and by the end of the ride, you will likely feel as if you accomplished only one thing: you survived. But was the risk worth the reward? If you felt afraid or anxious for the duration of the ride, did you get over your fear? No, you rode despite fear. The reward for that risk was not big enough.

Riding Fear Free says that it is no longer acceptable to feel fearful at any stage of the process, and the risks you will be asked to take will always be small and easy enough that you never feel pushed. Therefore, the risk is manageable at each stage. But if you also add rewards as you progress, you will start to enjoy the process more.

For example, if your ultimate goal is to canter in an open field, and you canter in the round pen while visualizing cantering in the open field, then reward yourself with something. The reward has to mean something to you, but it does not have to be huge or costly. Save the major reward for cantering in the field. If you enjoy quiet time, then set aside time to read a book, go look at the full moon, or schedule a massage. If you love shopping, get a new hoof pick or another small token of appreciation for taking the first step to overcoming your fear.

As the risks become harder, the rewards can increase. If you canter one step in that open field, you may choose to treat yourself to a new saddle blanket or a special night on the town. Again, this reward does not have to cost a lot of money, but it must mean something to you. Only you can determine the appropriate reward. Take time to evaluate and plan the risks and their meaningful rewards.

Over time, your rewards build on each other and have the additional benefit of helping you face the next risk. When you get to a more difficult part of the process, you have practiced enough risk/reward that you are subconsciously more willing and able to engage in the activity and change your pattern of thinking or behaving.

Notes

Part 2

Beyond the Basics: Becoming Fear Free

Five

Getting Started

Photo by Alicia Vander Meulen.

Evaluating Your Horse as a Fear-free Partner

Above all, fearful riders are horse lovers. Why else would they keep riding despite their almost overwhelming fear? Love is the only explanation. So hearing that you might need to part with your beloved horse is naturally painful.

But just as some marriages end in divorce due to irreconcilable differences, so do some horse-human relationships. Some people and horses are incompatible, and you should examine this possibility, especially if your fear centers on one horse in particular or if the horse has injured you repeatedly. In this case, fear may be your body's way of trying to keep you safe from that specific animal.

On the other hand, getting a new horse may not be the answer. Horses are not disposable, and it is unfair to go through one after another in the hopes of finding the one that will remove all fear. They are living creatures, they bond with their humans, and care should be taken in making the right decision for the horse and the rider and for the sake of finances.

To get an unbiased opinion on the suitability of a mount, consider requesting the help of a riding instructor or local horse trainer. Be sure to choose someone who has no financial stake in your choice. You need an uninterested party to give you an impartial opinion. If a new horse is chosen, you should not expect your fear issues to disappear. You still need to replace your fear memories with new, positive memories.

> Before walking through the gate on your journey to being fear free, make sure you have the right partners to help you along the way.

Illustration by Jim Bush.

The Unengaged Horse. Most horses are honest and straightforward, and they respond with energy and emotion. They startle when surprised or become nervous when facing unfamiliar obstacles; they show their feelings honestly without overreacting. But the unengaged horse seems to be okay with everything, even things that normal, well-trained horses would question. He will not have the usual reaction to surprises or unfamiliar sights. This horse may appear easygoing and bombproof, but in reality, he is just tolerating or ignoring the situation; he is not engaging or participating fully in the activity. His responses are so dull that most people mistake him for a "born broke" horse.

But just like the quiet neighbor or unassuming employee who one day starts shooting people at his workplace, the unengaged horse will "all of a sudden" react for no apparent reason, and the explosion will not be in proportion to the situation that caused it. Think of news interviews after a shooting. In every one, neighbors and coworkers say the shooter was always nice, polite, and easygoing, and they cannot believe he did something so awful. How could they not know his grievances? Because he never expressed his true feelings about anything, when he finally got overwhelmed, the response was out of control. The same thing happens with the unengaged horse. He will try to hurt himself or his rider in response to the situation. Why? The horse has never worked through his emotions, so he has no emotional control.

Lack of emotional control is also the core problem for fearful riders, who must learn to make their emotional responses proportionate to their circumstances, just like the horse does. In fact, emotional control is essential for all people and horses. If fearful riders are to overcome their fears, they need to work with reliable and honest horses. Pairing a horse that is not in touch with his emotions with a rider who is not in touch with hers can be a recipe for disaster.

Thus, the unengaged or passive-aggressive horse is the worst type of mount for a fearful rider. "Passive aggressive" does *not* mean the horse is "aggressive"—always charging, kicking, or biting; instead, he displays passive resistance to a handler by consistently maintaining an overall unenthusiastic attitude toward obeying cues. Rather than displaying his negative attitude or fear overtly—through honest reactions or even assertiveness or aggression in the moment—he ignores cues, responds slowly, or generally tries to avoid the activity. He shows his negative emotions in a passive manner by resisting the rider. Unfortunately, many fearful people are attracted to passive-aggressive, unengaged horses because they appear calm and non-reactive.

Characteristics of an Unengaged or Passive-aggressive Horse

• The horse does everything asked of him and appears perfectly accepting and trained, but his response to cues is slow, dull, and unengaged.

• He exhibits no energy or life in his response.

• He challenges the rider/handler over the same issues time and again. For example, no matter how much the rider has worked on canter departs, the horse resists them again on the next ride. He may kick out, wring his tail, or crow hop. His response may not be enough to hurt the rider, but he is still letting everyone know of his displeasure at doing that task. Except for these small shows of resistance, the owner considers him a well-trained, reliable, easygoing horse.

• The owner/trainer will use words like "born broke," say that he never had to give the horse much training, or claim never to have had a problem with him.

• The owner may claim that the breed is naturally slow, easygoing, or cold-blooded.

• The owner may say that anyone can ride this horse or that her children rode this horse from day one.

• It takes repeated, increasingly demanding cues to get the horse to do a simple, everyday task.

• Despite a solid training foundation, the horse resents doing simple jobs, resists cues, or reacts negatively when asked to do a basic task, like pick up his feet.

There are several ways to deal with a fearful rider/passive-aggressive horse combination. You can sell the horse and get one that better fits your needs, or you can choose to lease the passive-aggressive horse or put him in training with someone who understands how to teach a horse to engage in his activities and control his emotions. In this case, the fearful rider and the passive-aggressive horse will be on the same journey but not together.

A truly fearful rider should *not* attempt to work with a truly passive-aggressive horse. However, there are varying degrees of passive-aggressive horses and fearful riders. A mildly passive-aggressive horse may actually help a fearful rider, but special care should be taken in dealing with this pairing. Owners should honestly evaluate their horses. Do you have a horse that is mostly willing to participate and overcome his difficulties? If so, this could be a workable partnership. Or do you have a horse that goes from non-reactive to over-reactive with no middle ground in between? If this is the case, then the result will be injuries and heartache almost every time.

Not all calm horses are passive-aggressive. Many well-trained, relaxed horses are just what they seem: genuinely well-trained and relaxed. Do not make the mistake of over-sensitizing an easy, laid-back horse by spooking him until he responds. This will create a spooking machine. If you are unsure if your horse is passive aggressive, consult a professional trainer for an unbiased opinion.

Patriot: The Unengaged Horse

Patriot was purchased to be a family mount, and he seemed to be the ideal candidate. He never spooked and was always methodical in his responses, which seemed perfect for newer riders, and he was fun to ride. Children could pile onto his back and slide off his rump, and he loved to be groomed and even enjoyed pushing barrels around the arena. His gaits were slow and smooth, and he would stop immediately when riders practiced their emergency dismounts. Patriot was never aggressive or mean, but he was lazy. When he was asked to pick up a hoof, he would allow his handler to pick it up, but he wouldn't hold it up himself. He just leaned on his handler. When asked to work harder or go faster, he would swish his tail about the extra effort.

After years of passive-resistant behavior, Patriot started getting grumpy at saddling time, and then he began kicking out or pinning his ears when asked to lope, though he was not in pain from ill-fitting tack. Then, he started to pin his ears at other horses while on trail rides, and occasionally he tried to bite them, but overall, his behavior was still acceptable. Finally, on a trail ride, Patriot ignored his rider's cues and charged up a hill toward the lead horse, biting and kicking the other horse, unseating his rider, and startling everyone because the attack seemed to come out of nowhere. All along, Patriot had sent signals that something was wrong—that he was having trouble dealing with his emotions—but those little clues were easy to excuse as laziness or naughty behavior. In reality, Patriot had merely been tolerating his situation, showing disrespect for his riders, and not truly engaging in his activities, so when he finally reached his breaking point, his behavior was completely out of proportion to his circumstances.

What It Takes to Help an Unengaged Horse

When Laura's father gave her Anita as a birthday gift, the horse was only two years old. Anita was imprinted at birth, but then she was left with the herd to grow up. After running wild for so long, she was not tame and had to learn to be handled by humans, so Laura spent time teaching her the basics: how to accept a halter, lead quietly, and be groomed.

As training progressed, Anita began to display a pattern. First, she would try to avoid learning the new skill, and when that didn't work, she became aggressive, trying to make Laura give up. But Laura was persistent and would not stop, and finally, it seemed that Anita would come to accept each new lesson. In reality, though, Anita was often only tolerating the situation until she just couldn't handle it anymore. Once, as Laura was teaching her to accept being brushed, Anita stopped struggling, no longer pinned her ears, and finally cocked a hip in relaxation. Believing the horse was accepting her touch, Laura continued her grooming session until Anita simply couldn't take it anymore. The horse turned and bit her and then cow-kicked her, and this wasn't because Laura hadn't adequately taught the lesson to the horse or because the lesson was too difficult for the horse to handle. It was because the horse had been emotionally unengaged throughout the process.

Anita was Laura's introduction to unengaged or passive-aggressive horses. She spent many years working with Anita, and finally, Laura emerged as the herd leader. Together, Laura and Anita did it all; they rode English and Western, pulled a cart, rode bridleless, participated in parades, did trail rides, and even camped. Years later, Laura used Anita as a lesson horse, in 4H, as a show and trail mount, and eventually as a therapeutic riding horse. And even though Anita always had the tendency to ignore and resist, she became Laura's perfect horse, and this was only possible because Laura always made sure she was the leader and consistently corrected the horse for any attempt at resistance for the rest of her life.

(l to r) Anita and Laura's son Sean in trail class; Anita, Laura, and husband Dave at a parade; Anita and Laura's son Tyler in horsemastership class.

Illustration by Jim Bush.

Green Horse with Fearful Rider. The second worst type of horse for a fearful rider is a green or inexperienced horse. Traditional wisdom says that about 2,000 hours of saddle time are required to train a reliable riding mount. By the age of ten or twelve, the typical horse has had the requisite 2,000 hours. On occasion, a younger horse, usually a working ranch horse or a horse belonging to a trainer, may have accrued enough hours under saddle and been exposed to enough stimuli to be a reliable mount. And sometimes, an older horse may not have had the exposure and training to be a safe mount for a fearful rider. So age is not the most important factor in horse selection. Instead, consider a horse's number of riding hours and his breadth of experiences when selecting a mount for a fearful rider.

Because a green horse is still learning to be a reliable mount, it is unfair to expect him never to react inappropriately with a fearful rider on board. A seasoned horse can sense a rider's fear, and because of his training and exposure to various circumstances, he remains safe and reliable, but a green horse may become overwhelmed. Green horses are not bad; they simply are not ready to be reliable mounts as riders work toward becoming fear free.

If you have a green horse that is everything you want in a mount, you may not have to sell him. Instead, consider leasing a more experienced mount and placing your green horse with a steady rider who can help transform him into a great riding partner. When you are fear free, you can take over and put the miles and hours on your own horse, creating the reliable mount everyone envies.

Sassy: The Green Horse

When Abby purchased Sassy as a foal, she did everything right. She paid to have the filly handled by professionals, and when Sassy was old enough, she was professionally started under saddle and underwent months of training. Young Sassy knew all the basic cues and was learning fast, but she was still inexperienced, and her time with the professional trainer didn't expose her to every new sight she might encounter or prepare her for every task that she might be asked to tackle. Sassy was still learning about the world and what was expected of her, and she needed time to become a seasoned riding horse.

Fearful Abby was able to ride Sassy successfully under the supervision of trained professionals, but as much as she loved the young mare, she never felt completely safe and secure with her. She knew the horse was smart, honest, and well bred, and she always saw Sassy's future potential, but sometimes the mare would become excited or spook at new things. And finally, Sassy encountered a situation for which she was not prepared, and she reacted like any inexperienced horse might: by spooking and jumping sideways. Abby was unseated but physically unhurt.

But Abby was now afraid of her dream horse, and, worse, she realized that she might not be the best handler for the young mare. Fortunately, Abby made a wise decision. She began taking lessons on a seasoned horse and leased Sassy to a veteran rider who was able to help the mare gain the experience she needed. As Sassy matured and got more time under saddle, she lived up to the potential Abby had seen in her as a foal, and they have a bright future ahead of them. Fearful rider Abby and green horse Sassy had a lot to learn, and in order to reach their fullest potential, they had to take the same journey but not together.

Illustration by Jim Bush.

The Right Horse for the Job. Fearful riders need engaged, willing partners to help them on their journey. That doesn't mean that the horse has to be perfect, but it does mean that the horse has to express his emotions normally. A good horse has emotional balance. He is neither dull or over-reactive nor too slow or too quick to respond. He is an honest, emotionally engaged partner.

The right horse to help you is honest with his feelings, knows how to calm down after becoming emotional, and wants to participate in activities with you. The horse should do more than just tolerate you, and he should have the proper amount of training and riding time so that he will not be unduly influenced if you get scared.

No horse is absolutely perfect, and all of them make mistakes, but attitude and experience are critical. It will be easier for you to learn to manage your fears if your horse is interested in what is happening, obeys your cues, and is able to calm down quickly if something exciting happens.

Calvin: The Right Horse for the Job

At first glance, Calvin didn't seem like the perfect horse for a fearful rider. Sure, he was a mature, experienced show horse with years of professional training and saddle time, but he was also thin and had a stub of a tail, which he was constantly swishing. His owners rode him in a massive curb bit, tie down, and spurs, and his pain caused him to refuse to respond to their cues. Finally, Calvin was sold, and his whole life changed.

Gone was all the harsh equipment, and once Calvin realized that he was no longer in pain, he was able to return to being a happy, obedient horse. His jog was smooth, and his lope was practically a standstill. He was calm and focused while trail riding, herding cows, teaching special-needs riders, or doing arena work. Calvin loved children, and even though he was almost sixteen hands tall, he had a way of making himself small and approachable. He would lower his head and follow even the most timid child's every command. Though Calvin had flaws like any other horse, he was able to help fearful people because of his engaged and obedient attitude, years of training, and his breadth of experiences, all of which he could draw upon even if his rider became unsure.

Evaluating Your Riding Instructor or Trainer as a Fear-free Teacher

Even a quick look at the horse world today will reveal a plethora of big-name trainers (and plenty of lesser-known ones) who teach a variety of techniques from natural horsemanship to classical methods. Most of these training systems require the rider, first and foremost, to work around and help the horse. As a fearful rider, however, you need to learn how to help yourself first, and it may be too daunting a task to have to help a horse while you are learning to be fear free yourself.

Organized training programs are tempting for fearful riders. It seems as if all problems would disappear if you could just find the right method of working and communicating with your horse. But trainer and method shopping is not the answer. In fact, if you are trying every fad that comes along, you may be seeking ways to avoid facing the real problem—your fears.

In order to best help you become fear free, your teacher needs to understand the general principles of fear and how to extinguish it. They must agree never to push you and must allow you to be in control of your lessons. Finding a teacher may be difficult, but questions such as these will help guide you.

Does the Teacher

- understand fear and fear issues?

- agree never to push me?

- agree that I am in control of the lesson?

- seem willing to overcome his or her biases and do whatever it takes to help me?

- agree to flexible lesson plans?

- have a positive attitude?

The most important question of all is this: are you comfortable with your teacher? If so, you are ready to begin your journey.

Be aware that some riding instructors and trainers simply do not believe that fearful people have any business handling horses or riding them at all. If you discover a teacher who believes fearful riders are a "lost cause," then it is *not* your job to change that person's mind. Move on to a teacher who comprehends the strength required for you to seek help and who sees healthy fear as common sense in disguise rather than a weakness.

If you cannot find a teacher with whom you are comfortable, you can take the journey on your own. It will be difficult, but becoming fear free on your own is better than allowing yourself to fall under the influence of an unsupportive instructor.

The First Steps

Now that you understand the general principles of Riding Fear Free and have the right equine partner and teacher, it's time to get started.

As you prepare to strike off on your journey, you might find that the first step is the most difficult. How do you begin?

Take an emotional inventory. Before you begin to address your fears, you must be able to identify them clearly. This does not mean you must dredge up memories of what made you fearful, but it does mean identifying the moments when you become anxious while working with your horse. The following simple exercise will help you clarify what you are feeling as you work with your horse.

First, do what you would normally do with your horse. If you ride, then follow your regular routine. If you are not riding, that's okay. Do everything you would do on a normal day with your horse: grooming, groundwork, or even just watching him in the pasture.

Second, while the memories of your time with your horse are still fresh, write down exactly what you felt at each point in the day. Don't just focus on the negative feelings; also record your positive emotions. Every fearful rider needs to recognize both the situations that cause fear and those that cause joy or happiness. These positive emotions can become focal points and "safe places" to return to in order to build confidence and create positive memories. Make sure you note all levels of fear and the symptoms you experienced, from holding your breath to freezing and every variation in between. You are going to learn to be as perceptive with yourself as you are with your horse.

Consider having a trusted friend videotape your entire interaction with your horse. Be sure that your friend understands her role: to video the session and not to comment. She is just there to operate the camera. Later, you can watch the video as you do your emotional inventory. This will help you remember each emotion you experienced and will also have the additional benefit of letting you see what is actually happening at the moments when you felt joy or fear.

After you have recorded the emotions you felt during each part of your ride, it's time to analyze and determine which situations cause your fear. Overcoming them will become your end goals.

For example, you felt confident and happy while trotting, but you got nervous while cantering your horse. You have identified a comfortable situation and one that causes fear. Cantering fear free will become your end goal, and you will be able to write a lesson plan that takes you step by step from where you are comfortable (trotting) to where you are uncomfortable (cantering).

Write a Lesson Plan. While it may sound like you are going back to elementary school, writing a lesson plan is a good way to define your goal and help you to see the small steps you can take to reach it.

How to Write a Lesson Plan

(1) Define your fear issues using your emotional inventory.

Pick it apart point by point and write down each instance in which you experience fear. Remember that fear does not have to be full-blown terror; record moments in which you felt a bit off, even if you cannot describe it concretely. Note any type of resistance, hesitation, nervousness, or reluctance. Also remember that fear can also show itself in a lack of control, so you may find yourself taking risks or having too much bravado in order to compensate for your suppressed fear. Make sure to record this behavior as well.

Because you may have more than one fear issue to address, you may have to write a separate plan for each one. But you have to start somewhere, so choose one as your starting point.

(2) Define your comfort zone with regard to your chosen fear issue.

Work backward from your fear issue and hone in on the first place or first exercise that you can do with (or even without) your horse that causes you no fear. That's right. No fear. That is where you will begin. In the above example, the rider is completely comfortable trotting, so that would be the starting point.

(3) Define your final goal.

Leave a space in the lesson plan and write down your end goal. What do you want to be able to do fear free at the end of the lesson plan? In our example, the goal would be to canter fear free.

(4) Write as many steps as you can think of between your starting point (2) and your goal (3).

Starting with the exercise you are comfortable with, add a microscopic step. Then add another. And another. And another until you reach your destination. This is where your knowledge of horse training and riding will come in handy. You'll be able to adapt training exercises to help yourself. In the example above, you begin with trot work because you are already totally comfortable with trotting exercises.

In order to add steps to your lesson plan, you must ask yourself good questions about the exercise and your true feelings. If you already know you can trot easily and freely, then start there. But what next? Ask yourself these questions: Where do I feel completely in control at the trot: round pen, arena, open field? Where would I feel okay if the horse broke into a canter unexpectedly while trotting? By asking these two questions, you can decide the best place to start your trot and canter work. Once you choose the location, ask yourself less than/more than or easier/harder questions. What is easier than cantering but harder than trotting? Start at the easier task and move to the harder one.

Example Steps

• Find a safe enclosure such as a round pen, arena, paddock, or pasture that is free of obstacles and suitable for cantering.

• Trot a few strides, stop, and dismount. At this point, you need a total release. By changing your physical state, you reward your brain and body for your first fear-free accomplishment.

• Repeat the previous ride.

• Trot longer, stop, and dismount. Celebrate physically.

• Trot a few strides, stop, and *mentally* celebrate.

• Trot a few strides while thinking about/visualizing cantering. Stop, dismount, and celebrate.

• Trot a few strides and stop. Immediately, trot a few strides and stop again. Repeat. Dismount.

• Review your rides to this point. (Do not critique the horse or your riding, but review what you experienced emotionally.) Then, stop evaluating the ride and think about something else: chores at home or your upcoming day. Change your thinking as a mental release and then go back to riding.

• Add speed. Trot faster for a few strides, stop, and dismount.

• Add speed, trot faster, and stop.

• Add duration. Trot faster and longer, stop, and dismount.

• Add visualization. Imagine that you are preparing to canter and allow yourself to feel that emotion while you are trotting.

• When you feel ready, canter one stride, stop, dismount, and physically celebrate.

• Canter one stride, stop, and mentally celebrate.

• Canter two strides.

• Canter three or more strides down the short side of the arena.

• Keep building until you are cantering freely around the arena.

• Add small obstacles like cones, a clump of dirt, and ride to, around, over, and through them.

• As you freely canter in the safe enclosure, visualize cantering in the field, on a cross-country course, or on a mountain trail ride.

• Add barrels, poles, and jump standards to canter around, over, and through.

• Canter the obstacles, but pretend they are scary objects like trees to avoid, a deer jumping out of the woods, a fallen log to jump over, or a barking dog.

Be sure to stop and dismount whenever you move to the next major step in the lesson. This mental and physical break will help provide a release from the pressure of the last step.

If at any point in this lesson plan you feel fear, stop. Your subconscious is telling you to slow down. If physical activity does not make the fear dissipate, return to an easier step in the lesson and work that stage longer. Also consider adding additional steps between the easier step and the one that caused your fear or at any point in the lesson plan.

Notice that each step in the lesson plan constitutes a "new ride." The accumulation of all these short individual rides creates the new fear-free memories necessary to replace the fearful ones stored in the brain. The early steps of the lesson plan above emphasize the need to dismount from the horse even if you feel no fear. Even though your anxiety level is low, dismounting will keep you from ignoring your fear and letting momentum carry you through the scary activity. Taking a physical break also helps you focus on the small steps and not on the larger goal, which will cause you anxiety. Your activity keeps you from dwelling on the end goal of cantering, and you learn to ride in the present even as you work toward your ultimate, future goal of cantering in an open field.

The lesson plan above also gives teachers a brief example of how to use small steps to help students break down a lesson. Although it may seem excessive already, it is not uncommon for students to need as many as 100 steps between their starting point and the goal. The more you are able to break down the lesson, the more effective the teaching will be. With each new step, you can increase speed, duration, or distance. This incremental addition of physical and emotional challenges will elevate a simple exercise to one that truly addresses and involves the riders' emotions.

Lesson plans have a dual purpose. They provide a concrete plan to follow, and they also help you begin your mental preparation as you think through and plan your list of steps. As you record each step, you are already visualizing it. Riders will be tempted to let their professional trainers or instructors design the lesson plan, but it is much more helpful if fearful riders write the plan themselves. The writing of the plan is actually a valuable part of the becoming fear free. It begins to prepare the writer mentally for the physical work ahead. As you create the plan, you will have to think through and envision each step, and that forms the first layer of memory creation. Certainly, trainers can help by asking good questions and guiding the process, but their role is to *help* riders come up with the steps.

Lessons may be done in one session or stretched over several rides. There is no time limit, and it is important that if you feel fear at any stage in the lesson plan, you stop, go back to a step that does not cause fear, and work until you are ready to try again. If you think of additional steps in the middle of the lesson, feel free to add them before advancing to the next stage. The more you work your emotional gas pedal at the easier stages of the lesson plan, the faster you will reach your ultimate goal.

The difference between a good lesson plan and a great lesson plan comes in the flow of individual steps to reaching your goal. If the transition to each new step is logical and easy, it will not seem like you are doing something much different from the previous step. There should be no big leaps.

Beware of Patterns and Repetitions

Fearful riders often take comfort in patterns and repetitions. In fact, training and riding lessons are often based on patterns and repetitions because they establish a comfort zone. But what happens if you break the pattern or venture outside the comfortable arena? Sometimes things fall apart. Why? Because you have learned a pattern, but you have not learned what to do if the pattern is broken. Worse, the pattern can become an excuse for not working through your emotions. Dependence on patterns explains why some riders will not venture out of their discipline or ride another horse, but the best horses are cross-trained to keep them engaged and to teach them to manage their emotions in different circumstances. By riding a pattern, you may get comfortable doing one thing, but a fear-free rider will learn to handle anything, even something outside of his comfort zone.

Some highly trained horses have lived in a controlled world. They work in a soft, covered arena in a quiet barn where they can do tempi changes, but they quickly fall apart if someone breaks their pattern or routine. Rather than adjusting and changing the world around the horse, it is better to teach the horse to handle unexpected events.

The same is true for riders. Patterns give a false sense of security and may cause riders to believe that they are capable of handling more than they truly are. In reality, they have only worked through their emotions enough to get good at a pattern but not enough to control their response to every situation that might occur.

Of course, not all patterns and routines are bad. Using the same warm-up exercises and patterns can help settle both a fearful student and a horse having a bad day. They can also be used when going to a new arena or riding trail. Both horse and rider can draw comfort from arriving somewhere new but still doing the same routine that they do at home. Routine can help calm riders and horses in new environments, but relying on patterns alone will never help students become completely fear free or prepare them to handle an emergency.

Reaching Your Goal

After you have worked through your lesson plan and reached your goal, take time to process what has happened. Celebrate the accomplishment before looking forward to new possibilities.

Rider and Teacher Tips

Physical exercises are not the most important factor in helping riders overcome fear, but they do help people focus on each step toward the goal of riding fear free. The real transformation comes from the rider's ability to adapt and change his or her thinking during a ride. Do not make the mistake of adhering to a rigid plan or memorizing a pattern. Instead, use surprises and interruptions to your advantage. As riders learn to adapt to easy interruptions, they are preparing to think through and adapt to sudden surprises or true emergencies.

Notes

Six

Keeping a Journal

Photo by Laura Daley.

Keeping a journal may seem like an unnecessary part of learning to ride fear free, but if you agree that overcoming fear involves changing the way your brain perceives horse-related situations, then you are already aware that most of the hard work is mental—retraining the brain—and not physical—retraining the body.

> Most of the hard work necessary to ride fear free occurs off the horse.

Reading and writing are just as powerful as riding. Researchers have discovered that reading certain words activates not only the language centers of the brain but also other parts as well. For example, words like "lavender" or "cinnamon" activate the smell centers of the brain, and words like "leap" or "skip" activate the motor cortex—the brain's motion center (Paul, "Your Brain on Fiction"). The brain reacts similarly whether we actually do activities or merely read about them, so writing and rereading journal entries are ways to create real fear-free memories in the brain.

Because much of the work to become fear free takes place in the brain, where you can replace your fear memories through visualization, the journal actually supplements and serves the same function as your riding time. The journey to riding fear free is not about physically attaining a goal, such as cantering in a field, jumping a fence, or going to a show. The journey is about learning to do these things without fear. So, while you need to address physical riding skills and practical horse-training aspects, the primary focus should be your emotions. A journal is a helpful tool for learning to capture thoughts, ask good questions, and see the reality of a situation.

But there are many excuses for skipping this step: you don't think you're a good writer, you can't spell, you don't have time, etc. But the fact remains that processing and releasing your emotions is a key to becoming fear free, so find a way to do that. If you absolutely refuse to write, consider investing in a recording device or dictating to your phone or computer. Just find a way to express your journey in words and record your progress.

Your journal offers you the opportunity to express all your feelings without judgment. You can write anything without needing to filter yourself; you can be brutally honest, raw, and open. No one will understand your journey as well as you, and by pouring out your experiences, thoughts, and actions, you will be able to process them in a safe manner. Reading your journal will give you a glimpse at the inner workings of your own heart, and you will eventually learn to tame the thoughts and emotions that you once believed to be automatic and uncontrollable. Just as video allows riders to see what is happening physically, a journal allows you to see what is happening mentally—your thoughts and emotions.

How to Use Your Journal Effectively

After each fear-free training session, spend time recording the lesson in your journal. Take an emotional inventory after each lesson. Write down what you did and how you felt about what you did. If your anxiety started before you got to the barn, then begin writing about where you felt the first emotion.

It will be tempting to bypass the journal in favor of talking to friends or family about your lessons. It is natural to want to share experiences with these people, who have traditionally been your means of support. But the goal of *Riding Fear Free* is to help riders learn to process and evaluate their own emotions rather than leaning on the opinions of others who may not truly understand what they are experiencing. Venting or sharing your feelings with friends, relatives, or even other horsepeople may make you feel better for the moment, but it can also end in frustration when you receive unwanted advice or criticism. Besides, it will not get rid of your fear. In fact, talking to others about your issues can actually be a way of avoiding the hard emotional work required to become fear free. You need to process your feelings, evaluate them, and let them go. Writing in a journal helps you do that.

Using Your Journal for Self-reflection

Processing and Releasing Emotions. Your journal is the safest place to process and release your emotions. As you begin to record your lesson experiences, sometimes new emotions will surface. But with distance from the activity, you can look at the experience from a different perspective and evaluate how you reacted and why.

Other emotions, such as anger, sometimes mask fear. In the learning process, people may need to deal with these emotions. Fortunately, they can use many of the same techniques for dealing with fear to deal with other emotions. The most important aspect of confronting any emotion is that the rider learns to acknowledge, process, and release it.

But why wouldn't people want to express their emotions, especially the positive ones? It could be that they do not like the loss of control that comes with honest emotion. Since childhood, they may have been conditioned not to overreact or look silly in public. They may have been shamed into hiding behind the image of the good or perfect child. As a result, they suppress rather than express their emotions, be it fear, anger, resentment, or even too much joy.

They may have experienced a childhood trauma and now block themselves from feeling their emotions, thus stopping their feelings from working correctly. Because they cut off their emotional lives completely, they have also lost their ability to control the intensity of their reactions once they begin to feel again. The first few times they try to express their feelings, they will be out of control.

Recognizing Themes. Keeping a journal gives you insight into your thoughts and patterns of behavior. By reviewing your journal, you will be able to recognize patterns in the ways you think about and react to the situations you encounter with your horse. You may discover that you are a perfectionist and become discouraged, depressed, or angry when you make mistakes, or you may find that you are prone to "what-if" thinking when you ride in certain environments. These insights will help you recognize your thoughts and behavior patterns while they are happening, and then you will be able to make a conscious choice about how to manage them.

Aiding in Positive Self-talk. By reading back through your journal, you will be able to see a visual representation of your thinking. As a result, you will also recognize negative thinking while it is happening and turn your thoughts in a positive direction. You will learn to see when and why you are hard on yourself, and then you can reexamine the situation and find something positive in the worst moments.

Rider Tips

You may find it difficult to write in your journal, but your effort will prove worthwhile. Your journal will not only provide insight but will actually create new fear-free memories without requiring you to be in the saddle.

Providing Insight for Teachers

Teacher Tips

Your student is taking a risk by trusting you to read his private and emotional journal entries. Your role is not to critique his spelling, writing style, or even emotions but to help him see the positive in his worst fears or what he perceives as a bad ride.

Reading your journal will help your teacher better understand your fears. It will also provide the opportunity for her to correct misconceptions and misunderstood lesson steps. But your journal will not be graded like a school assignment. Instead, a teacher's comments should become a source of further support and encouragement.

Teachers can magnify the effects of a student's journal by offering written feedback. The most effective method of doing this is to correspond via email with students. After each lesson, your teacher may ask you to send a copy of your journal entry if you feel comfortable doing so. Your teacher will not critique your writing or correct your spelling, but will read and respond to your questions and point out areas you might have overlooked.

Seven

Seeing Reality

Photo by Laura Daley.

In a dangerous situation, fear is a friend. Fear is the brain's way of preparing the body to react to unsafe conditions. But fearful riders experience fear that is not proportionate to their circumstances, and, to make matters worse, they feel anxiety long after the danger has passed. To get rid of anxiety, riders must replace their fearful memories with positive ones. But how do fearful riders keep their brains from overreacting in the moment?

Because fear is not a conscious choice, it seems as though it would be impossible to change the way riders naturally react to their circumstances. But that is not true. It is possible for fearful riders to develop emotional control. In fact, the human brain has a built-in emotional control center: the rostral cingulate. When the amygdala is busy generating fearful emotions, the rostral cingulate is working to moderate them. Subconsciously, the brain is already analyzing what is happening and helping the person to react in proportion to the threat. Riders can help the process along by making the conscious decision to ask good questions about the reality of their circumstances.

> Did this horse sit down on the side of the mountain or is something else going on? Fear can skew reality, causing the situation to seem out of balance and off kilter. Riding fear free means learning to see what is really happening around you.

Asking Good Questions

Fearful riders are usually hyper-aware of everything going on around them. Consciously or unconsciously, they notice when the horse's tail moves, when he tenses his back muscles, and even when the wind blows or the neighbor's dog barks two blocks away.

Any one of these things could be enough to cause anxiety in fearful riders, and they may or may not realize exactly what causes them to feel fearful in the moment. They just know that they are scared.

At this point, it is important to learn to ask good questions about what is really happening. During any lesson or ride, if you find yourself feeling uneasy, stop the lesson and ask yourself questions like these:

- What is happening around me?
- Am I truly in danger, or am I engaged in what-if thinking?
- Can I do something easier than what I am doing to lower my fear level?
- How do I see myself in the world? Around horses? Around other people?
- Is what I feel in proportion to what is happening?
- Is what I feel based on fact or emotion? Is it true?
- Is this line of thinking helping or hurting my ability to ride and interact with my horse?
- How can I turn this mistake or problem into a positive learning experience?
- If I continue on this path, will my relationship with my horse improve or worsen?

Reality TV

Video is a good tool to help you see what is really happening during your interaction with your horse. Videotaping an entire lesson, not just the riding portion, will give you a clearer picture of what is going on both physically and mentally. You may not realize that your anxiety is triggered when your horse is slow or refuses to pick up his feet. Even before a ride begins, you may become anxious after the horse pins his ears when you approach with the saddle. Other riders may be able to ignore these issues, but they raise the anxiety level of fearful riders. Viewing footage of your time with your horse will help pinpoint exactly when your fear or anxiety begins and what causes it to escalate.

As you watch the footage, you will be tempted to critique your riding or your horse's training. Instead, use the videos as tools to help you see what is truly happening around you. Instead of being critical of your riding, focus on your emotional reaction to the events you see. Compare what you wrote in your fear journal to the events in the video and notice when you felt fear and how you dealt with it. You will likely see that your reaction to certain events was out of proportion to what really happened. Being able to recognize this disconnect between reality and your brain's perception is the first step in seeing reality in real time and reacting accordingly.

Anticipating vs. Living in the Moment

Humans are unique in that they are the only creatures who have the gift and curse of anticipation. That means people have the pleasure of looking forward to something pleasant but also the misfortune of being able to dread something unpleasant. More important for the fearful rider, humans have the ability to manufacture scenarios that may or may not happen in the future. Riders can wonder "what if."

Fearful riders often use what-if thinking to imagine the worst-case scenario possible, thus activating their fear even if their true circumstances don't warrant it. For example, a slow ride around a pond on a peaceful day could turn into a fear-inducing experience if the rider allows herself to wonder what might happen if a duck flew out of the vegetation. As a result, the rider begins to anticipate the duck flying out and becomes nervous. The horse picks up on the rider's fear and becomes fearful too. So in essence, a pleasant, calm ride is transformed into a scary, difficult ride because of the way the rider thinks.

In fact, many fearful riders spend their time in the saddle wondering what if. What if the horse spooks? What if the horse rears? What if he jigs? What if he won't stop? When a rider's mind races with what-if questions, it is helpful to give it something to race to: answers.

Riding Fear Free encourages you to challenge and change your negative what-if thinking through various methods, such as asking good questions or even acting out the what-if scenarios. The problem with what-if thinking is that it takes you out of the moment—out of your true circumstances—and puts you into the worst-case scenario. The truth of the matter is that you can be in a safe, calm environment, but you feel as if you are in life-or-death danger. Because you can't fix what you don't know is happening, the first step in combating this problem is to become aware of your thinking patterns. As you ride, make it a point to evaluate your thoughts. Are you wondering what would happen if...?

If so, then ask yourself what is causing you to have this thought and feel this fear. Is your situation dangerous? Do you even see a flock of ducks? If your situation is dangerous, then you can take steps to make yourself safe, such as dismounting and approaching the ducks from the ground while leading your horse through groundwork maneuvers. If your situation is safe, then this is the time to practice another fear-free technique.

Because your body language changed the moment you thought of the what-if scenario, your horse went on high alert too. In order to help lower your horse's anxiety, do a controlled spook by purposefully startling him with a small noise or motion. By

Teacher Tips

Try to help the rider realize when she is over-thinking and over-analyzing a situation and help her change the course of her thoughts. Have the rider act out or verbalize the what-if situation she fears.

recognizing your horse's anxiety and choosing when and where he will release it, you are able to take control of both your fear and your horse's. This will also bring you both back into the present moment.

Once the extra energy is released, try a technique such as distraction or visualization as you ride around the pond. Sing, concentrate on a riding maneuver, or do something else that will help you change your thinking. Try to visualize riding in the round pen.

If you cannot distract yourself or visualize yourself elsewhere, then it's time to think about what positive actions you would take if your worst-case scenario happened. Instead of dwelling on what-if questions, answer them instead. What would you do if the frightening scenario actually happened? What would your actions be? You should remind yourself of the tools and exercises in your training toolbox. Develop a plan and practice it as you ride.

When you begin asking what-if questions, taking physical action will help prepare both your mind and your body for the would-be emergency. By choosing where and when the what-if happens, you are taking control of the situation. By practicing what you would do in a safe place, you are building muscle memory in order to deal with a real emergency in the future.

Examples of Turning What-if Questions
into Positive Responses

What if my horse spooks? If your horse spooks, what do you normally do? Do you disengage the hindquarter? If you decide that is the best reaction, then practice it while in a safe place. Would you do an emergency dismount? If so, practice that. Or practice doing both in sequence.

What if my horse jigs? You can always dismount and do ground exercises with the horse. Choose tasks that challenge the horse's mind; do not simply lunge him in a circle. Take control of his feet by asking for rapid changes of direction and speed. Do changes of gait, turns, serpentines, or other exercises that control the horse's speed and direction. As the horse settles and begins listening, slow the pace and soften the requests.

What if the horse throws his head? Go directly to one rein and ask the horse to bend his head around and lower it. If the horse continues to toss his head, disengage his hip to a complete stop and dismount. Go to a safe area and teach the horse to give to pressure until he will drop his head with little or no rein pressure. Then, get back on and resume riding.

What if my horse runs away? To deal with a runaway at speed, do an anchoring rein stop (sometimes called pulley rein), which is similar to a one-rein stop. However, the addition of the anchor hand helps to balance you and prevents you from over-bending the horse, causing him to become unbalanced. Place your hands on both reins and sit deep into your seat. Take the slack out of the right rein and anchor it to the horse's mane just in front of the saddle. Once that hand is locked down, take all the slack out of the left rein. When you can feel the horse against the bit, raise your left hand straight up in the air until the horse stops. This action will bring the horse's nose in and down to the left, off-setting his head and putting it more in a position to listen to the stop cue. Practice this exercise enough to know the procedure (muscle memory) but not so much that you make the horse resentful. This is a shutdown demand that tells the horse to stop his feet, so be careful not to drill it too much.

Notes

Eight

Advanced Visualization and the Benefits of Distraction

Photo by Laura Daley.

Advanced visualization is more than just having good thoughts, thinking positively, or envisioning good outcomes, although a good attitude does help people overcome horseback-riding fears.

Visualization is a favorite technique of self-help gurus, who espouse an imagine-it-to-receive-it ideology, but the type of visualization that helps eliminate fear involves more than just thinking happy thoughts and expecting to receive rewards from the universe. A person's subconscious mind cannot tell the difference between visualization and reality, so what is seen in the mind is as valuable as actual, physical experiences.

Envisioning a perfect ride creates real memories in the subconscious mind to replace old fear memories, but that is only one reason visualization is so valuable to the fearful rider. When combined with physical simulation or practice, visualization becomes even more powerful and beneficial. Visualization allows you to ride where you can while you imagine riding where you can't.

> You can create new fear-free memories by imagining yourself riding in the wide-open spaces while actually remaining in the safety of your own arena.

Visualization for Overcoming Performance Fears

Most people are familiar with visualization as a technique for improving athletic activity and overcoming performance anxiety. Before an event, professional athletes often close their eyes and make the motions of their sport. They are envisioning their event to help improve their performance while physically practicing the motions.

When utilizing this technique for overcoming performance anxiety, it is vital to replicate the exact circumstances in your mind. Visualize the crowd. Hear the noise. Feel the excitement. Make the movements. Smell the hot dogs and fly spray. The more realistic the images in your mind, the more beneficial the exercise.

Professional equestrians ride patterns in their minds successfully hundreds of times before they do the physical ride at a big show, but that doesn't mean they stop practicing the physical skills and rely solely on visualization exercises. Science has shown that visualization can help improve simple motor skills, but in order to maximize the results of the technique, riders must combine visualization and actual practice.

Overcoming Riding Fear in the Comfort of Your Own Home

You don't need to be on your horse, or even at the barn, to begin overcoming your fears through visualization. All it takes is a quiet moment of focus. Like the athlete before a competition, close your eyes and imagine your perfect ride. Imagine in as much detail as possible. Feel the weight of the saddle in your hands as you approach your horse. Hear the leather creak as you lift it to his back. Imagine the exertion of your leg muscles as you mount your horse while he stands perfectly still. Feel the sensation of the sun on your back and experience the rhythmic sway of your horse's stride as you walk onto the trail. Smell the flowers, and breathe deeply the wonderful scent of the horse. Hear his footfalls as you move into the trot. Feel the wind in your hair (below your helmet, of course).

There. You have just mentally experienced a perfect ride, and your fear memories are losing power, but in order to improve the effectiveness of visualization, it is necessary to add a physical component.

Still, you do not need to leave home.

Consider purchasing an exercise ball—or drag it out of your closet—to use as your virtual horse. The ball should be sized so that it will allow you to approximate your riding posture comfortably. It should be large enough so that your knees are not overly bent, but not so large that you can't sit balanced with both feet on the ground. Exercise balls are usually measured in centimeters and are available in a fairly large range of sizes (55-85 cm). Manufacturers often print a handy chart on the box so that you can choose the correct size ball for your height. When in doubt, get a larger size. You can't make a small ball larger, but you can under-inflate a big one.

With your new virtual horse, repeat the same visualization exercise, but add the physical movements. As you imagine mounting, mount your virtual horse. Gather the virtual reins in your hands. As you imagine walking down the idyllic trail, move the ball as if your horse were walking. Feel the swivel of your hips and the way your weight shifts with each step. Then, move into the trot and change the virtual horse's gait. Experience the bounce of the trot as you go lightly down the trail. Now, you are physically and mentally experiencing the perfect ride.

Adding the physical movements to the visualization exercise will allow you to create good mental memories to replace the fearful ones, and these feelings will be reinforced throughout your entire body. Visualization on your virtual horse will also create new muscle memories that will improve your seat, balance, and core strength.

Adding Video. Set up your virtual horse in front of the TV or computer and watch videos of other people riding. Choose videos that show rides you would like to replicate once you are fear free. Watch professionals ride their dressage tests, complete reining patterns, or even jump courses. Watch cowboy racing, cross country, or cutting. And as you watch, ride your virtual horse through the same patterns and obstacles. Be the rider on the video. Let the ball move as the horse moves. Change gaits with the video. As you do this, you are creating many memories of perfect rides to replace old fear memories.

If you have video of you riding, watch it as you ride your virtual horse. This will probably be more challenging because you will be tempted to critique your riding. Try to resist this temptation. Just focus on feeling your horse's movements beneath you.

Visualizing Negative Experiences to Help Overcome Fear

Many people advise fearful riders not to dwell on the experiences that caused them to be afraid or to think of the situations that make them feel anxious. But, once you learn to ask good questions and control your emotions, you can use these negative experiences as valuable learning tools. Visualizing negative experiences or reliving accidents or traumas can actually change the way your brain works if you deliberately choose to create a positive ending, avert the disaster, and take appropriate action. During memory reconsolidation, when you are actively recalling the fearful moment, you can choose whether to reinforce the negative memory or change it by creating a positive outcome, even if that's not literally what happened. The brain does not differentiate between actual experiences and the memories of it, so you are literally changing the chemical processes in the brain by creating a new ending in your mind.

As in the previous exercises, you can use visualization on your virtual horse to help you deal safely with the emotions that arise in an emergency situation. Begin by visualizing a situation that causes you anxiety, but do not start with a big wreck. Visualize the events that lead up to the scary moment. What is the horse doing? What are you feeling? What is happening around you? Move your body along with the horse as he reacts to the situation. Feel the fearful emotions and take the steps to avert or deal with the problem. By creating a positive ending to the situation, even if you are reliving and changing a true story, you will help loosen the fearful memory's hold on your brain and literally begin altering the way your brain reacts to the stimuli you imagined. Instead of feeling disproportionate anxiety and freezing, you will feel the correct amount of anxiety for the situation, and you will be able to react appropriately.

Visualizing traumatic experiences may not be pleasant, but in addition to taking away the power of the old, fearful memories, it has two enormous benefits: this exercise allows you to practice raising and lowering your emotions in a safe place, and it helps you to practice the physical steps you need to take in order to keep yourself safe in such a situation. So you are preparing both your mind and your body to react more appropriately in a real emergency.

Adding Video. After visualizing fearful situations that you have experienced and giving them new endings, consider adding video. Begin by watching videos of safe riders doing things that cause you fear. Ride your virtual horse along with the videos, and when you feel ready, consider riding along with videos that involve accidents or falls. As you ride with these videos, concentrate on what you would do differently in reaction or to divert the accident altogether. Practice the correct response on your virtual horse.

More Ideas for Effective Visualization at Home

• Watch horse-training videos as you replicate the movements on your virtual horse.

• Practice riding patterns and doing gait transitions on the virtual horse.

• Imagine emergency situations and practice the correct response to them.

Taking Visualization to the Barn

Visualization is not only helpful at home; it has myriad practical applications at the barn and even under saddle.

To begin, it's not necessary to mount your horse. You don't even have to get him out of his stall. But you can do all the visualization exercises mentioned in the previous section in the presence of your horse. You will actually be able to experience the barn atmosphere and smell that delicious horsey smell as you imagine your ideal ride. You don't have to do anything special. Just sit outside your horse's stall and enjoy your perfect ride on your perfect horse.

Watching Others. This is akin to adding video to your home visualization exercises. Only now, you can watch horses and riders in real time. Sit on the sidelines of a dressage or reining lesson, or watch as a pleasure rider enjoys his horse as they ride down the driveway together. Imagine yourself riding along with them on your perfect horse.

When a mishap occurs, this is a good thing, although it may not seem like it at the time. It is important to raise your emotions and learn to calm down afterward, and watching a spook or crow-hop from the sidelines is much safer than being on the horse's back when it happens.

The Virtual Horse at the Barn. This may seem silly, but consider bringing your virtual horse to the barn with you. This will give you yet another step in the visualization process before you get in the saddle. If you feel comfortable, use the ball as you go through your perfect ride visualization in the presence of your horse. Continue adding physical motions to help build muscle memories along with new fear-free memories. Just as you did with the virtual horse at home, move along with your horse. Cue your horse. Feel your body as it balances with each step. This is adding another dimension to your fear-free memories.

If you feel uncomfortable or are unable to bring your virtual horse to the barn, you can achieve the same benefits by walking your course as you visualize riding it. While the virtual horse may provide a more accurate feel of riding, you can actually practice the same movements on foot. Practice walk/trot transitions as you make them yourself. Imagine striking off at the canter on the correct lead as you lope off on foot. You can practice even the most advanced dressage movements and reining spins on foot as you visualize them.

You can use these visualization techniques whenever you enter a new riding environment. For example, if you are going to a new trail-riding facility and are feeling nervous, you can bring the ball along with you to "ride" outside your trailer as you absorb the sights and sounds of the new location, or you can walk the trails or arena as you visualize yourself on your horse. And as you become more confident, you can lead your horse as you walk along beside him and imagine yourself in the saddle.

This will acquaint you with the new facility and give you (and your horse) fear-free memories from your first "ride" there. When you finally mount your horse, you will already have many successful rides under your belt.

Watching Others and the Virtual Horse. The next step in the progression is to ride along on your virtual horse or walk along beside as you watch others enjoy their horses. This may be an intimidating prospect, but a strong support system of riding buddies or trainers will understand that this exercise will result in long-term fear-free riding. Seeing and experiencing the emotions of another rider will help you practice raising and lowering yours, ask good questions, and develop positive memories so that when you are ready to mount your own horse, you have hours of confident rides and practice sessions to draw from.

Ride Where You Can...

John Lyons's axiom to ride where you can and not where you can't is a valuable lesson for fearful riders. This means that people should ride only where they are comfortable. If you feel safe in the round pen but begin to get nervous in a larger arena, ride in the round pen and continue doing so until boredom compels you to move to the arena. When you are bored in the arena, move to a pasture. When you are bored in a pasture, move to an open field. And if you get nervous in the arena, pasture, or field, visualize riding in the round pen where you felt safe. Continue until you are completely fear free no matter where you are.

Many fearful riders resent the idea of staying in a safe place when they really want to learn to ride the trails or gallop cross country. They may still feel the pressure to "just do it" or "cowboy up" and open the gate too soon in the process. This is understandable. Surely you can't get over your fear of trail riding by walking along a round pen.

Or can you?

Illustration by Jim Bush.

...But Imagine Riding Where You Can't

Using visualization, it is possible to begin creating new fear-free memories of riding where you can't. You can ride in a pasture, you can ride at the National Finals Rodeo, and you can ride on the side of a cliff or in the desert or at the Olympics. Just use visualization.

Extinguishing fear requires the rider to accumulate many fear-free memories to replace the old, negative memories, and the best way to begin this process is to use visualization under saddle. The mind will accept these new visualized memories as valid replacements of the old fearful ones, so when the time comes to open the gate and ride outside the round pen, you will have already done it hundreds of times in your mind.

This is a powerful technique, and it can be used throughout a riding career and not just for beginning fearful riders. Here are some examples of how visualization under saddle can help riders of all fear levels.

To use this technique, choose a place where you feel completely safe to ride. Begin with your warm-up exercises and stay only at gaits at which you feel comfortable. This is not the time to push. This is the time to visualize. Once you feel comfortable in your physical location, begin to visualize your "goal location." Perhaps it is a trail ride, or maybe it's the larger arena next door. It doesn't matter.

As you ride in your safe location, imagine you are going farther. See yourself in the big arena. Imagine the feeling as your horse walks down the long side of the arena. Practice stopping your horse at different points. Practice riding exercises that you would use in the larger arena to slow or stop the horse in an emergency. As you ride, see yourself in the "scary" location, and to your mind, you will be there physically.

Replicating Obstacles. As you progress in your mounted visualizations, you may begin to wonder about what might happen if you come upon an obstacle or a scary object. The great news is that anything you can do outside can be replicated in the arena.

Although this technique falls under a "riding" category in this book, you don't have to be in the saddle to do these exercises. Begin by leading your horse across the obstacle, and take to the saddle only when you feel completely ready. It may take many practice sessions on the ground before you are ready to mount. This may seem discouraging, but remember, you are creating good memories for both you and your horse and are practicing valuable groundwork skills.

You are also reminding yourself that when you encounter an obstacle in the real world, you always have the option to dismount and work the horse from the ground until he is willing to cross calmly. While many riders believe that leading a horse across an obstacle constitutes a failure on their part or means that they have "lost a battle with the horse," this is absolutely untrue. If you or your horse become nervous about crossing an obstacle, then the best thing to do is to start where you are both comfortable and approach and retreat until the horse will cross willingly and without fear. Remember, the goal is for both you and the horse to cross the obstacle fear free. Do not lead a fearful, reluctant horse across any obstacle. If the horse is in a fearful state, he may injure his handler if he is pushed too hard too soon. If the horse is not walking calmly on a loose rein beside you, then do not try to lead him across the obstacle. Use approach and retreat until the horse is willing and calm before tackling any obstacle from the ground or in the saddle.

You may begin replicating obstacles in the arena without using physical objects at all. Just use your visualization techniques. See a water crossing ahead. How would you ask the horse to cross it? How would it feel when he successfully waded across the creek? Practice your rein cues to keep the horse lined up properly and your go-forward cue to ask him to step across.

This rider uses a box to simulate a scary trail obstacle. By using this object in combination with visualization, she creates new fear-free memories, practices the physical skills necessary to cross the obstacle, and reinforces the horse's trust in her leadership.

Photo by Laura Daley

Then, add a physical obstacle. Start small and build from there. Draw a narrow line in the dirt, and imagine that you are crossing a trickle of water. As you begin to cross a trickle of water confidently, make the line bigger and imagine that it is a small creek.

Use a pole, a twig, or a patch of grass to simulate any obstacle you think you might encounter in your daily riding. It doesn't matter what object you use to create the obstacle. Just begin by guiding your horse across the object and imagining the real-world impediment it represents. Use the same cues to cross the obstacle, but imagine you are crossing something much larger. Then, use a larger obstacle. This time, try something like a large sheet of plywood or an old piece of carpet.

The physical act of creating each obstacle while imagining it as a real-world jump, water crossing, or low-hanging branch will help you create positive memories without even having the horse nearby. And gradually making the obstacles more challenging will allow you to improve the skill and build more fear-free memories through visualization. Practice obstacles will also raise and lower your emotions in a safe situation. Remember that the goal is to learn to *control your emotions* while you jump, cross water, or avoid a branch.

The most amazing thing about combining visualization with obstacle replication is that while you are building many fear-free memories for yourself, you are also building them in your horse. With each successful pass over a scary object, you are reminding your horse to trust your judgment and to follow your cues. So when you come to the physical water crossing, your horse will already have many memories of you guiding him safely across an obstacle, and he will be more ready to accept your guidance.

> **Rider Tips**
>
> Visualization and distraction are tools that you can use for the rest of your life. Any time you feel yourself becoming tense or fearful, you can visualize yourself in a different situation or distract yourself until you are able to calm down.

Riding at Your Goal but Visualizing Riding in the Round Pen

All that practice riding in the round pen is going to come in handy when you finally make it to your big goal: the show ring, the cross-country course, or the trails. Once you get to your final destination, you may start to feel some of the old fear. One way to combat it is to visualize yourself riding in the round pen. This will help center you and prepare you for your ultimate goal of riding fear free.

Visualization can be an infinitely useful tool. You can use it to practice raising your emotions in a controlled environment by imagining yourself riding on a precarious mountain peak while actually walking around your arena. Conversely, you can use visualization to lower your emotions when you are in a less controlled environment by imagining yourself back in your arena when you are actually riding that mountain peak. No matter what your situation, you can use visualization to help control your emotions.

Visualizing Negative Events and Releasing Fear

If a traumatic accident is a source of your horseback-riding fear, then after you have begun to develop new fear-free memories and have learned how to control your emotions more effectively, you may choose to recall your accident and deliberately change its effect on your brain by imagining a different ending and a positive outcome. This exercise may be difficult, so it is vital to begin in the comfort of your own home and not around your horse. If you don't yet feel comfortable remembering your specific accident or if a traumatic event is not the cause of your fear, you can still help build new fear-free memories by visualizing what-if scenarios.

Imagine your what-if scenarios or remember the traumatic event that triggered your fear. Feel everything: the saddle underneath you and the reins in your hand. Hear birds chirping, cars going by, or a whinny. Feel the sun on your skin. Relive your memories of the scary event, but create a new ending in which you avert disaster and are unharmed. Then stop and realize that you have remembered all this while you are safe and sound in your home.

Next, sit on your virtual horse and relive the same fear-inducing event with its new, positive ending, adding the horse's movements too. After feeling your fear, return to the safety of your house.

When the event is no longer causing your fear to increase to its former levels, you have developed even more emotional control. Head to the barn and do it all over again next to your horse's stall or while watching someone else ride. You will experience the sights, sounds, and smells of the barn, but you are not actually on a horse.

With practice, you may even be able to sit on your horse and relive the fearful moment or to ride as you recall it and its new conclusion. This last suggestion is not necessary to be fear free, so only go there if you want to do so.

The Benefits of Distraction

Visualization and distraction are two sides of the same coin. When you have already asked good questions about your situation and have decided you are safe, but you still feel anxiety, distractions will help change your frame of mind in a positive way. You are keeping the mind from going into the what-if/anticipation mode by actively choosing to think of something else.

Talking. Talk about your day, pets, spouse, children, family, or friends. It doesn't matter what you talk about as long as it prevents you from over-thinking or over-analyzing what is happening in the ring. Avoid discussing what is going on in the ring or during the lesson. If your anxiety level allows it, you can also use your own voice to remind yourself of the steps to an exercise. Speak each step aloud as you do them. You can also gauge your nervousness based on your voice. Does it crack or get high pitched as you ride and work your horse? Do you whisper or shout as your horse moves around or takes a sudden side step? If you have any change in tone or modulation, you are in need of some other distractions.

Singing. Singing is a great distraction. You do not need special equipment, just your voice and willingness to sing even if it is off key. Singing instantly regulates your breathing, and the right song can transport you out of the arena and into a relaxed or motivated state. Songs used in movies can capture not only your hearing but also your imagination, making you feel a little more daring and excited for the next step in your lesson plan.

Listening to Music or Audiobooks. Like singing, listening to music can both inspire and calm you. You may also benefit from the words of an inspirational speaker, recordings of relaxing sounds, or even audiobooks. Listen to your favorite trainer or comedian. This can stop your what-if questions and give your mind something better to focus on.

Notes

Nine

Physical Relaxation Techniques

Photo by Laura Daley.

Riding Fear Free offers techniques that address the whole rider—mentally and physically. Both facets of the rider must be addressed in order to become fear free. This means addressing physical pain and tension both while riding and in everyday life. The exercises in this chapter not only teach body awareness, flexibility, and relaxation but are also useful as a routine to help you to warm up slowly and quietly before a ride or to work out the kinks afterward.

> Learning to relax physically will benefit both you and your horse.

Body Check

Joints. Assess the way you feel by rotating and flexing every joint. This should not be a twenty-minute workout but rather a quick check of how you are moving that day. Using slow and sweeping movements, flex every joint one at a time, and ask yourself how each area of your body feels as you move it.

Working from head to toe, check every part, including your eyes, jaw, tongue, and fingers, and work all the way down to your toes. As you go, be sure to take deep, cleansing breaths; your lungs need checking too. This exercise will help you discover where you hold tension. Are you stiff in your ankles, do your shoulders ache, or is your back stiff? Consider doing a daily body check, especially when you plan to be with your horse.

Rider Tips

Are your socks too tight in your boots? Is your bra supporting you correctly? Is your fancy new moisture-wicking shirt causing you to sweat more? Find out what may be causing you discomfort and annoyance and get rid of it immediately. Even minor irritations can affect how you ride or work with your horse.

Muscles. Similar to the joint check, you can also assess your muscles by tensing and relaxing each group. Start on one side of your body and work from your head to your toes. Then switch to the other side. Contract each muscle tightly and then relax it completely.

As you practice this exercise, you will become aware of soreness in certain muscles, which means you have either overworked a muscle or that you hold tension there. This retained tension will become clear at other times during the day as well. When you feel stress, you can purposefully overtighten these already tense muscle groups and then relax them. The more often you check your muscles, the more in tune you will become to the way you hold tension in your body. And the sooner you can identify your tension, the sooner you can release it.

Calf Stretch

Fearful riders often have issues with tight, short calf muscles. If you put your heels down in your stirrups, but they seem to pop right back up, then your calves have not been stretched enough to stay comfortably in a heels-down position. If you are a woman who often wears high-heeled shoes, you will have to work harder to condition and strengthen your calves so your heels will stretch down while riding.

Stand on the balls of your feet on a raised platform about two inches tall. Allow your weight to sink back into your heels, stretching your calves. Do not bounce, but stretch slowly. Gradually increase the distance of the stretch by standing on taller platforms such as railroad ties, fence rails, or a step.

Tendon Stretch

Tight tendons can cause people great discomfort, but they are often overlooked as the source of the pain. Stressful situations and prolonged sitting can cause tendons to tighten. How can you tell if your tendons are tight? Follow the length of a major muscle, like your calf, toward a joint. Do you feel a tight cord over the muscle or just below the surface of the skin near your ankle? That's your tendon. When you press it firmly, it should give to the pressure. If you feel resistance (or if it doesn't give at all) to your palpation, your tendon is too tight.

In order to release the tension in the tendon, find the ends (heel and knee for calf tendon) and work them as if you were sawing them with the side of your hand, or pluck and roll them until they start to give to your pressure. Check the tendons in legs, thighs, arms, and shoulders. Learning to release your tendons will give you a more relaxed and easy ride on your horse. (For more information, see Meyners, *Rider Fitness*.)

Mounted Warm-up

While sitting on your horse in the middle of a safe enclosure, align your body, placing the ear, shoulder, elbow, hip, and ankle in a straight line, and sit correctly for your saddle type. Keep one side of your body in the correct position while working each joint of the other side — starting at your toes and working to your head — using the same techniques as you did in your body check. Make your movements sweeping and slow so you do not become unbalanced; however, you may find yourself leaning or even unable to move a particular part of your body. Do not strain. Over time, you will become more flexible.

You can even include your horse in the warm-up by having him walk along the rail after you have learned all the exercises at the halt. Have the horse travel counter-clockwise as you warm up the left side of your body and clockwise as you work the right side of your body so that you do not hit the fence as you do the exercises. Once you are comfortable doing this warm-up at a walk, try them at a jog, trot, and lope.

The Benefits of Massage

You do not have to get out your checkbook and schedule a professional massage in order to reap the benefits of it. The simple act of touch can help pull the negative energy out of a muscle group. By feeling tightness or soreness in your muscles and rubbing it away yourself, you can be an effective masseuse for yourself.

Combining Visualization and Massage. The purpose of this exercise is to visualize negative horse-related events while physically reminding yourself to relax at the same time.

Schedule an at-home massage or ask your spouse or friend to help you with this physical relaxation technique. Let the masseuse know that the purpose of the massage is to help you visualize negative events while keeping your body relaxed. This is more of a workout for your "fear muscles" than your literal muscles. If you do not feel comfortable engaging the help of someone else, then you can do the physical massage yourself.

Find videos of scary, traumatic, or even normal horse activities while getting a relaxing massage or doing it yourself. This serves as a physical reminder to relax and not tighten up during a scary event.

Releasing Tension

Physical relaxation is about more than stretching and warming up. You can also ease tension in the middle of a lesson by doing certain physical actions to release it.

Laughing. Laughter is not just good for the soul. It also helps you release physical tension. If you feel fear coming on, try a good belly laugh. This will often pull you out of fear mode. If you can't laugh, then do something to reengage joyful emotions. Watch a comedy movie or read a humorous book. You *can* gain control of your emotions when you feel fear taking over by using laughter.

Shaking It off. The term "shake it off" is not just a saying. You can release tension by deliberately shaking the excess energy from your body. When you feel tension or fear, shake yourself from head to toe.

Celebrating Life with Energy. Part of riding fear free is learning to celebrate every achievement—small and large. This celebration should be both a mental assent that you have done something praiseworthy and a physical action to help release any lingering tension: jump, laugh, or move in some other way. This type of celebration will be difficult for some people, so you may want to start in the privacy of your home. Remember how you expressed joy when you were a child and had not developed inhibitions that occur with adulthood. Make yourself vulnerable and try to feel alive and free spirited. Start small and build your celebration until you express everything you feel.

Engaging All Five Senses

Has a memory ever come flooding back to you after you smelled a certain perfume or heard a song on the radio? That memory was anchored by one of your five senses. Memories can be connected to sight, smell, touch, taste, or hearing, so in order to create new, positive memories based on old, fearful events, it is important to get all your senses involved in the process. Changing input to one of your senses can disengage you from the power of fear memories.

Sight. Ride with sunglasses. Close your eyes while riding in the arena. Take videos of yourself and others. Watch professional tapes or online videos. Changing the way you see the world or exposing yourself to more images of horses and riding is more than just visualization. It uses your sense of sight to create new memories in your brain.

Sound. Hum, sing, or play music while working with your horse. Music can be both calming and energizing, and you will begin connecting positive memories with the songs you choose. Also consider using rhythm beads, bells that attach to your horse's tack. They calm you as well as your horse.

Smell. Use essential oils or choose a different perfume (or no perfume at all if you always wear it) for your time at the barn. Scent forms one of the strongest memory connections in the brain, so look for creative ways to bring new smells to the barn.

Touch. A change in texture can also help in firmly establishing new, fear-free memories in the brain. If you wear gloves, stop; if you don't, start. Change your usual riding attire by putting on a t-shirt under your riding shirt, tie small knots in the lead rope, add tape to your reins, or put dots of glue on the backs of your brushes to make bumps.

Taste. Try using peppermint, cinnamon, or wintergreen mints or gum as you work with your horse. Don't forget to blow bubbles as you ride. Also consider sweet-and-sour candy or two-flavored gum so that the taste changes as you ride or work your horse.

Sensory input can also negatively influence your ability to enjoy your whole equine experience. Certain sounds or smells can turn a normal ride into an irritating event, so watch for things that may annoy you or even be maddening to you. Reevaluate your tack, clothes, and equipment, and eliminate or replace the products that bother you so that you can experience a more pleasurable ride.

Teacher Tips

Engage all your students' senses with simple additions or alterations to your lesson equipment. Change your lesson tack by putting colored electrical tape on brushes, reins, or lesson props. Exchange leather reins for cotton reins, or add perfume or essential oils to the saddle pad or to the horse's mane. Such changes do not have to be expensive, but they will help riders create new fear-free memories.

Notes

Ten

Sample Fear-free Exercises

Photo by Laura Daley.

Riding Fear Free is designed to provide general concepts that fearful riders and their teachers can apply to their specific circumstances; it is not meant to be a rigid lesson plan that must be followed closely. This chapter contains some ideas for applying the general techniques in the first part of this book in order to ride fear free.

The goal of every rider—from the least fearful to the most terrified—is to become increasingly more at ease in different situations. Horse-related fear comes in many shapes and sizes. Some people enter the horse world almost unwillingly. Perhaps you are the parent of a horse-crazy child, and you must learn to overcome your fear of horses to help make your child's dreams come true. Or maybe you are a seasoned rider who has been in an accident, or you have always been timid or anxious. You may no longer be able to move or function as an able-bodied rider due to age, disease, accident, or injury not related to horses. There are so many degrees of fear and variables in the person's final objectives that providing a concrete step-by-step lesson plan is difficult.

This chapter offers ideas for using some traditional exercises in combination with *Riding Fear Free* techniques to extinguish fear.

> Trying new horse activities can help build fear-free memories.

Expanding the Comfort Zone

Why It Works: Uses pressure and release to increase the activities a rider can do without inciting fear.

The rule—begin where you do not experience fear—still applies. If you are too anxious to stand beside the horse or even in the same barn with the horse, then it is necessary to start wherever you feel comfortable. That may mean beginning beside the horse, five feet away, or outside the barn.

Once you are positioned within comfortable proximity to the horse, then you should find a place to sit and read. Your task is to absorb the atmosphere: hear the sounds of the horses as they walk around their pastures and smell their scent. But you should keep your mind focused on other, pleasant things.

This is the beginning of good memory creation. Even if you are not thinking about horses or challenging yourself to get closer, you are developing positive memories. You are getting used to the sights, sounds, and smells of the horse without having to address your fears head on.

With each visit, you should be encouraged to get closer to the horses only as you feel comfortable. It may take time, but you will be able to watch more and be closer to the horses without feeling anxiety.

Making a Horse-show Mom

Her daughter was the most horse-crazy child ever, and this devastated Erin, who was so terrified of horses that she couldn't even make herself pull her car all the way down the barn's driveway, much less stand at the rail of the arena to watch her daughter's riding lessons. Her fear of horses was so overwhelming that she had to drop her daughter off a quarter of a mile away from the barn.

Still, Erin was desperate to enjoy her daughter's equestrian passion, and so she began her fear-free journey at the spot where she felt no fear: a quarter of a mile away from the horses. At each of her daughter's lessons, she would drive only as close as she felt comfortable, roll down the windows so she could hear the barn activity and smell the horses, and then distract herself with reading or knitting. If she became nervous or fearful, she went home immediately.

With each trip to the barn, Erin was able to pull her car closer until she could park in the same lot as everyone else. Eventually, she began to build from staying in the barn parking lot for only a few minutes before becoming fearful to staying for an hour. By beginning where she felt no fear and gradually expanding her comfort zone, Erin created a firm foundation for the rest of her fear-free journey, and by using a combination of other *Riding Fear Free* techniques, she eventually became a true horse show mom by learning to groom, braid manes, and even load and haul horses in a trailer.

The same concept applies to many riding exercises as well. By staying in your comfort zone until you are bored or feel ready to move on, you can gradually move your riding area from a round pen to a large arena to a field. Or you can move from walking to trotting to cantering to galloping. The possibilities are endless for expanding your comfort zone.

Ups and Downs

Why It Works: Uses approach and retreat to expand the rider's comfort zone and can be combined with visualization to replace fearful memories with positive ones.

Photo by Laura Daley.

Any time you are in the saddle, your brain interprets it as a full ride and thus creates a new memory to help override your fear memories. The brain understands mounting, sitting for five seconds, and then dismounting in the same way it understands mounting, walking five miles, and dismounting. A ride is a ride, no matter how far or how long it lasts. So the first ride for any fearful rider should be nothing more than a mount followed by a dismount. Up and down.

The time in the saddle should gradually be elongated, and the full exercise should be repeated until you feel no fear. The up-and-down technique can also be combined with distraction and visualization. If a teacher is present, she can help you relax by asking distracting questions. These questions should not be horse related; they are meant to keep you from fixating on the what-ifs of the situation.

While you are in the saddle, you can begin visualizing your ideal ride. Imagine it in detail and say it aloud to the teacher. Many sports psychologists suggest visualization as a way of overcoming performance anxiety. By imagining what the ideal ride would be like, competitors essentially practice their routine or course in their minds, creating good memories even if they did not literally, do the sport. By combining ups and downs with such visualization, you can create memories of ideal rides without taking one step.

You may think this exercise sounds simplistic and silly, but it is an important and useful tool in your fear-free toolbox. Perhaps you will not need many ups and downs before you are ready to move forward, but you should be aware of this exercise so that you can use it again if you find yourself in a fear-inducing situation as you progress toward riding fear free. You should practice the exercise in non-stressful situations so that it will automatically leap to mind as an option if you start to feel anxiety. At any time in the future, you will know that you can change your state of mind simply by using ups and downs.

For example, let's say an already fear-free rider is going on his first off-site trail ride. It is new for both the horse and the rider, and even though they have prepared by doing many of the exercises in this book, they feel nervous. Anxiety in a new situation is natural, and it is an opportunity to use the up-and-down exercise to create fear-free memories in the new environment and to help the rider prepare to move forward and face other challenges without experiencing fear.

The rider will be focused on riding down the trail, but he cannot walk down the trail if he is not prepared to ride in the new environment at the halt. So the first ride at a new place might also be an up and down. Get on, sit, and then get off. Celebrate a successful ride. Repeat until the rider is ready to ask the horse to walk a few steps.

Short Rides

Why It Works: Allows riders to accumulate hundreds of good rides to replace negative fear memories in a short time.

Much like ups and downs, this exercise emphasizes short amounts of time in the saddle and many repetitions. Start with deliberately short rides. Mount, take one step, dismount, and then celebrate the good ride. Repeat it. As with ups and downs, the actual time in the saddle is less important that the repetitions. Good memories are built by repetition, not endurance.

As you progress in your fear-free journey, you will be able to break rides down mentally, without actually dismounting and remounting. The brain interprets every mental unit of the ride as a new ride, so one ride becomes many short rides without the rider having to dismount and begin again.

This is another exercise that can be used again later in the fear-free journey.

Leading a Mounted Rider

Why It Works: Replaces fear memories with positive ones and allows the rider to practice capturing thoughts or asking good questions without having to worry about controlling the horse.

Enlist the help of your teacher or another trusted helper, and begin this exercise at the halt. Do ups and downs until you feel ready to start the leading exercise. When you are comfortable, ask your leader to take one step forward and then stop. Add one step at a time until you are walking consistently in a straight line, but remember to keep each ride short and dismount in between. As you progress, you can incrementally add duration by making rides longer, gradually increase difficulty by including large sweeping turns, or add speed one step at a time. You may also try riding with your eyes closed and describe what is happening around you as you are being led. What do you hear and smell? What do you feel? Then open your eyes to see the reality of the situation. You may lose your sense of balance when you close your eyes, and you may start tipping to the side without realizing it. Open your eyes occasionally to make sure you have not started to lean. Soon, you will be able to judge your own straightness with your eyes closed.

Keep these sessions short and ask good questions throughout the process.

Follow the Leader

Why It Works: Replaces fearful memories with positive ones, distracts riders from fearful thoughts by allowing them to concentrate on the leader, and builds muscle memory.

Follow your teacher or another rider, and mimic everything she does. Follow her exact path, ride the way she rides, and move the way she moves. Begin with simple exercises, including straight lines and large circles at slow gaits, and build to more advanced maneuvers, such as crossing obstacles or even jumps.

The leader should ride correctly but also provide examples of incorrect riding for you to follow. This will help you learn what it feels like to be right and how your body feels when you are out of balance or doing something wrong.

Reciting Lesson Steps

Why It Works: Reinforces the lesson plan, teaches riders to ask good questions, and helps them celebrate each small accomplishment.

Recite your lesson plan as you work with your horse or ride. This can bring comfort because you will be familiar with exactly what will happen, and it can serve as a tool to help you remember all the steps. This is especially helpful if you do not have a teacher. Be your own best cheerleader, and don't forget the accolades and positive self-talk as you ride.

Doing One Thing

Why It Works: Establishes a safe zone or activity to return to during times of stress.

Remember those riding lessons when it seemed like there were too many things to worry about? Chin up, heels down, shoulders back, inside rein, outside leg, half-halt. And do it all at the same time. Rather than trying to do everything all at once, find one thing you can do well and build on it. Stop trying to ride the whole horse and control only one part.

Once your chosen action becomes automatic, it is your safe zone. You can return to that one exercise and perfect it if you are having a low-confidence day or your horse seems unsettled. You do not always have to learn something new. Sometimes going back and perfecting something simple helps to build confidence and restore balance.

Picking Where You Are Going to Die

Why It Works: Takes riders' worst fear to an absurd level but in a safe environment, helping them learn to capture their thoughts and control their emotions even in the worst circumstance. Helps riders take control of their fear.

Many riders have a fear of dying as a result of a horse accident. If you experience that feeling but you are in a safe area, then find the perfect spot to die. Yes, you read that right: pick a spot in the round pen, field, or arena where the horse is going to dump you. Make sure that it is nice and soft, and ride to it. Once you arrive at the perfect dying spot, decide that it is not the ideal site to land after all and pick a new spot. Keep picking different locations around the arena until the fear of falling is not as overwhelming.

This may sound like a counter-intuitive exercise because you are activating your fear of falling, but by choosing where the theoretical fall happens, you are taking control of your fear at the same time. This keeps your mind working and helps you control your emotions while you are in safe circumstances. Meanwhile, it makes falling seem less scary.

But wait! *Riding Fear Free* says never to ride when I feel fear. Why is this riding exercise recommended when someone is clearly afraid of falling? The most important prerequisite for choosing this lesson is that you are safe—the horse is calm, the arena is safe, the circumstances are controlled—at all times, but you are still afraid of falling. If you feel afraid of falling because you are in a dangerous location or in uncontrollable circumstances, then you should dismount and practice this lesson where you are safe. This is where the ability to ask good questions comes in handy.

If you have questioned yourself, and you realize you are on an obedient horse in a safe area, but you continue to fear falling even after asking good questions, using visualization, and practicing ups and downs, then this is the exercise for you.

Taking the situation to the point of absurdity is a good way to deal with irrational fear. You have already used logic to determine that you are safe, but the nagging fear of falling and dying lingers and you cannot rationalize it. Therefore, it is time to address the issue head on. This exercise allows you to act out the fear and replace it with good memories.

This exercise can be amplified and improved not only by riding to a new spot to die but also by actually stopping, dismounting, and sitting or lying in the spot. As you sit or lie on the ground, decide that it's not so bad to be on the ground, but it's still not the right place to die. Get back on and ride to another soft spot in the arena. Dismount and practice sitting or lying down as if you had fallen. As you step off the horse, practice tucking and rolling with your momentum, rather than bracing against the fall. Do not practice thudding to the ground on your tailbone; instead, sit down and continue to roll while tucking your arms to your sides. This will both address your fear of falling and begin introducing the skill of falling safely.

The only difference between this exercise and your fear of falling is that in this exercise, you came off the horse in a controlled manner and picked where and when it would happen. Acting out your fear in a controlled manner—and surviving—helps the brain process and release it. And because speed is the only difference between a real riding accident and the "accidents" you've practiced, you are also preparing your body for a real emergency. The actions are identical. As you learn to relax and go with the movement and momentum, you are actually learning to come off the horse at speed. You are neither fighting nor bracing against the fall, so the chance of getting hurt or breaking bones is greatly reduced. This exercise works on both a mental and physical level in order to prepare riders to deal healthily with the accident they fear.

Teacher Tips

Watch students for any signs of fear. If they are hiding fear in order to make progress, then it is your job to explain the goal: to feel and process fear and not to accomplish something physical.

Building Confidence through Muscle Memory

Why It Works: Allows you to practice any general fear-free principle while also building muscle memory and increasing familiarity with the horse's movements.

Rhythm. Do this exercise in a round pen or small enclosure on a trusted horse. Jog or trot on the rail while extending both arms forward and even with your shoulders. Raise and lower your hands with the rhythm of the horse's front feet. If you cannot match his footfalls, put your hands on the horse's shoulders and say "left, right" as you feel the rhythm. Practice until you can start and stop your movements in time with the horse's rhythm at any point.

Next, practice moving your hands in time to the horse's hind feet and continue until you can start and stop your movements in time with them too. Then, practice alternating between the front feet and hind feet.

When you feel ready, try it at the lope. Using your inside shoulder, circle your arm in time with each stride. One complete arm circle should occur for each lope stride.

Rein Adjustment. This exercise teaches you to adjust your hands along the reins no matter what your horse is doing. Once this exercise is perfected, your hands will never freeze, and you will not use the reins for balance.

Begin at the halt. Keep your core centered over the horse and your hands in a four-inch square around the pommel of an English saddle or the horn of a Western saddle. This four-inch zone is the optimum place for maintaining balance and control. Drop the reins on the horse's neck, pick them up, and adjust them to the correct length. Practice with one hand and then the other, and, finally, use both together. Close your eyes and repeat. Try it while sitting in an awkward position. Even try it while sitting backwards. Find and adjust your reins until it becomes second nature.

Sliding off the Horse. This exercise builds confidence and trust in your horse, but before trying it, make sure that your mount is accustomed to having someone slide off all sides, including his rear. It is not only fun to use a horse as a slide but also

Photo by Laura Daley.

wise to condition him to this exercise so that you can dismount safely from any position without scaring him. Start by hanging over your saddle and then sliding down the side. Or sit correctly and dismount by swinging a leg over the horse's neck and sliding down on your backside. Shift your body out of the seat and behind your saddle and slide off the horse's rear. By sliding down the horse, you will be more confident that your horse will let you dismount in awkward positions.

Around the World. This exercise builds confidence and balance. Sit on your horse at a halt in the round pen, and have someone hold the reins if necessary. With arms stretched to your sides like airplane wings, swing your left leg over the horse's neck. You are now sitting sideways in the saddle. Then, swing your right leg over the horse's hindquarters. You are now sitting backward in the saddle. Next, swing your left leg over the horse's hindquarters to sit sideways in the saddle facing the opposite direction. Last, swing your right leg over the horse's neck to return to a normal riding position.

When you start this exercise, you may find yourself unable to swing your legs freely over the horse's body, so try lifting your legs as high off the saddle as possible while staying seated and imagining that you are turning. Often, fear and tension, not stiffness, keep you from completing the exercise. Practice until you can circle left and right and are comfortable moving all over your horse. If you feel yourself falling during this exercise, just slide off the horse as you did in the previous exercise and mount again. This too will help you get comfortable in odd positions on your horse without becoming fearful.

Building Confidence through New Activities

Why It Works: Raises and lowers the student's emotions in a controlled environment and adds an element of fun.

Photo by Vicki Strickland.

Follow the Leader to Chasing a Cow. Chasing builds confidence in a timid horse and rider. Following another horse and rider, tracking a ball, or even chasing water sprayed from a hose can be a fun way to introduce a challenge that quickly builds confidence.

If the horse has not been introduced to the ball, do so on the ground. Begin by rolling a ball away from the horse and leading him toward it. Slowly, lead him closer and allow him to touch the ball. As the horse's confidence increases, encourage him to kick and chase the ball. Before mounting, be sure that the horse is accustomed to seeing the ball roll toward him and not just away. A horse that is confident chasing something may startle if it suddenly comes after him. This chasing exercise can be expanded to include tag, chasing the teacher, rolling a barrel, or tracking a cow or chickens. Start slowly and build energy.

Dropping the Reins. Many fearful students have trouble developing trust in a horse and may feel out of control if they do not have direct contact with the horse through leg and rein aids. Build a foundation of trust by standing at the halt and letting the reins rest on the horse's neck. You may want to begin by having a teacher or friend hold the horse. Work up to walking in a round pen while the reins rest on the horse's neck. Or have someone lead you. If the horse is reliable, consider riding in the round pen at a jog or trot and lope or canter.

Riding Bareback. Sitting directly on the horse's back, with no saddle, can help you become accustomed to the finer movements and muscle shifts of a horse's body. You may need to start by leaning against and hugging the horse and then progressing to standing on a mounting block and resting your weight on his back. When you feel ready, mount the horse and ride at the halt. Feel the horse breathe and the way his muscles move as he shifts his weight and looks around. Progress to the walk if you feel comfortable

Vaulting. Once you are comfortable walking bareback, try simple warm-up exercises or yoga on horseback. Try the body alignment warm-up routine in chapter 9, simple stretches, or even Around the World as you ride bareback at the walk. You do not have to become a true vaulter or have a wide-backed horse to do simple maneuvers.

Conclusion

Any riding or training exercise can be used in conjunction with the general principles of *Riding Fear Free* in order to help extinguish fear. The better you understand the general concepts of memory replacement and pressure and release, the better you will be able to apply them to any exercise you know. Just be sure that you follow the main rule of riding fear free: if you feel fear, stop immediately. If you ride with fear, you are reinforcing it.

Eleven

Becoming Fear Free: A Rider's Perspective

Photo by Laura Daley.

The journey to fear free begins and ends with you, the rider. You are the only person who can make the decision to change. You must find the right resources or teachers, and you must do the work. It sounds like a daunting task, but the good news is that you are in control of your future, and your future can be fear free.

> Fear-free riders are thinking, assessing, and questioning riders.

Trust But Verify

Many of the exercises in this book might seem too simple—or even too silly—to be useful, but they have been proven to work time and again, and they are supported by scientific principles. If you understand and agree with the concept of memory replacement for overcoming fear, then you realize that you must begin where you feel no fear and create good memories from that point. It may seem ridiculous and even a waste of time and money to have a full lesson of just mounting and dismounting a horse, but if taking one step forward causes you fear, then it is the best to start with the basics.

During this process, you may be asked to do other things that adults ordinarily wouldn't do. Perhaps you'll be asked to sing in order to help your breathing or jump up and down to release tension. You will probably feel self-conscious, but try to tap into your inner child. At least give it an effort.

One of the keys to success is "trusting the process" by taking part fully in each exercise and continuing until you learn the lesson. This type of trust in the process is important, but even more vital is that you trust the process *and* verify it.

Test the theory. Research it. If something seems wrong, question it. One of the reasons people become fearful is that they have lost the ability to think through their situation and see reality. Some have stopped questioning completely and defer to instructors or trainers to tell them what to do and when. That is not riding fear free.

Fear-free riders are thinking, assessing, and questioning riders.

As you take your journey to riding fear free, try to resist the temptation to dismiss a technique or idea or to follow it blindly. Study the concept behind the exercise first, and then, if it makes sense, give it a try. Experiment and assess afterward how it worked. But only do something if you are 100 percent comfortable with it.

Being Ready to Change

> Are you willing to live in fear forever? If not, then you have already taken the first step to riding fear free.

The process of becoming a fear-free rider begins when you decide that you are ready to change. This sounds obvious enough. You are tired of fearing the thing you love most. Besides, no one enjoys living in fear, and it seems like few people would willingly remain in that state. But like those who stay in unhealthy marriages or abusive relationships, some people seem drawn to chaos. No matter how often they have been injured—mentally, physically, and spiritually—they fear change more than they fear their current situation.

Change can be scary because it leads us into unknown territory and makes us ask tough questions. Is it really possible for me to ride without fear, or am I naturally more timid than other riders? What will the process be like? Will I be pushed into doing things I don't want to do? Will I end up making my situation worse?

But the most important question to ask is this: Am I willing to live this way forever?

If the answer is no, then you have already taken the first step to riding fear free.

Willingness to Work

Before you can begin to learn to deal with your emotions, you must be willing and ready to make a change. This means more than mental assent to the idea of change. It means a willingness to work hard and try new techniques and ideas, even if they sound silly. It means being willing to explore emotions and to be vulnerable. It means being open to changing almost anything: ill-fitting tack,

Jennifer and Darcy

Even though Jennifer made a living telling stories, her journey to becoming fear free depended not on inspirational tales but on cold, hard science. She spent years believing her fear meant she was deficient as a rider and even as a human being, so she had a hard time grasping that simple actions—like using short rides to create new fear-free memories—could change what she thought was her natural state. No amount of stories about other riders' past successes could convince her otherwise.

Before Jennifer could take the first step on the fear-free journey, she had to do the research; she had to understand the concepts behind everything that was asked of her. She wouldn't agree to do something without knowing *why* she was doing it. After reading numerous science articles to learn how the brain deals with fear, she was able to invest wholeheartedly in the fear-free journey.

Armed with her new understanding of fear as a physical process that takes place in the brain rather than a sign that something was amiss in her character, Jennifer began taking short rides, writing in her journal, and using pressure and release on herself in order to condition her brain to respond to a scary situation in a new and positive way. Even though she is not yet taking her dream trail rides in the Appalachian Mountains or galloping in open fields, she has gained something more valuable. Jennifer has the knowledge and skill to take each step in her fear-free journey as it comes, and soon, she will be doing things she never dreamed of trying.

(l to r) Darcy catnaps at Jennifer's first off-site trail ride; Laura and Darcy before a fear-free lesson; Jennifer's first fear-free canter in an open field, which Laura captured on video.

poor training techniques, unproductive riding habits, negative riding partners, and even negative thoughts.

Nothing in the world—including the best horse trainer or this book—can help someone who does not already want to change and who is not willing to do the work that is required.

But for those who are truly ready to release fear, the journey begins with a commitment to change and work at correcting behaviors that are counterproductive to fear-free riding.

Finding the Right Teacher and Understanding Your Role in Lessons

Unfortunately, it can be difficult to find trainers and riding instructors who have experience dealing with fearful riders. Most have probably helped restore the confidence of already confident individuals, but few have dealt with truly fearful riders and even fewer have made it an area of focused study.

If you cannot find a person who has experience with fearful riders, choose the teacher with whom you feel the most comfortable, and be clear about your fear issues and what you expect from your lessons. Select someone who has a positive and joyful attitude, and avoid serious, competitive instructors and trainers who approach lessons with a gruff mentality, which will hinder your progress. Make sure your teacher is willing to work at your pace and not merely instruct you as you follow a rigid lesson plan through constant drilling or exercises.

Organizations that certify riding instructors can help you find a teacher who may better understand your fears. Search websites of certification programs, such as the Certified Horsemanship Association (CHA) or the Professional Association of Therapeutic Horsemanship International (PATH), for local listings of approved teachers. Be aware that not all certified teachers use the methods in this book, so question them carefully. It is better to have a non-certified teacher who understands the concepts in this book than a certified teacher who does not.

The most important aspect of the teacher/student relationship is that the student is *always* in control of the lesson. *You* can choose to stop or slow down at any time. If you start to experience fear—or even begin feeling uncomfortable—you can and should stop the lesson.

This runs counter to what most people think. They see the traditional model of the teacher giving instructions and the rider following her, and that is fine if the lesson is to teach someone a physical skill or task. But you are doing something different. You are learning to process and release your fears. And while the teacher is there to guide you and support you, she is not there to push or drill you.

Fortunately, reading this book will help you understand the process and empower you to make wise decisions on your journey, but you must also find an instructor who agrees with the concept of turning over control to his student, using memory replacement for overcoming fear, and working toward fear extinction. Make sure you are comfortable before committing to lessons with any trainer.

Changing Riding Partners or Supporters

When you decide it's time to overcome your fears, people will give you advice, and much of it will directly conflict with what *Riding Fear Free* teaches. Some well-meaning friends will think their advice is helpful, and others will see and undermine your success by belittling your accomplishments. Just like alcoholics and addicts cannot always keep the same friends if they truly want to change their habits, sometimes fearful riders in recovery will find it helpful to distance themselves from negative influences—even if the negativity is unintentional.

> Fearful riders need positive riding companions, and negative influences need to be left behind.

Once you reach your goal, you may be able to reintroduce these friends into your riding circle, but there is nothing wrong with limiting your exposure to negative attitudes while taking the journey to riding fear free. If you cannot remove yourself completely from a negative person, then agree not to talk about horses while working through the process. Just as you choose not to discuss politics and religion with some friends, you can choose not to discuss horses for a time too. This includes virtual friends on discussion boards and social media websites and even family members. Sometimes riding alone is better than riding with the wrong people. But the best situation is to find positive, supportive friends with whom you can celebrate the tiniest accomplishment.

Dealing with Bias

Everyone in the horse world has an opinion about the best way to ride, the best discipline, the best training method, the best breed of horse, and even the best way to clean a hoof. This is natural. We gravitate to certain objects and techniques based on our history and personal preferences.

As you begin your journey to riding fear free, it is important to be willing to put aside your biases, which can become roadblocks on your path. Don't allow your personal preferences to keep you from moving forward. Once you have become fear free, you will also be free to return to your preferences.

Photo by Lauren Daley

Tack. Often, fearful riders are encouraged to try a more secure saddle. Many people are advised to choose a rough-out seat or switch to a western saddle for more security. The idea of using a saddle for security may be distasteful to you. After all, isn't it true that good riders are balanced and don't rely on their saddles to keep them safe. That might be a good argument if we were discussing riding technique and not the fear-free journey.

While you are working to overcome fear, it is important to use all the tools available to you, and there is no shame in making a tack change to keep your body safe and to put your mind at ease as you work toward your goal.

Discipline. Similar to the advice to switch tack is the suggestion to change disciplines. English riders might be advised to try a more relaxed Western discipline, and Western riders might be told to try English techniques, such as posting or cavaletti, to help develop balance or confidence. The idea of a change of discipline might make you uncomfortable, but you should consider this: a saddle is just a seat, but good riding is good riding.

Don't let yourself be turned off by outer appearances or accessories. Your ideal teacher may wear breeches or cowboy boots. Your lessons might take place in a fancy mirrored arena or in a riding pen surrounded by cattle pastures. Your perfect horse might wear a slick dressage saddle or silver-studded western rig. Keep an open mind, and remember that you aren't there to learn a discipline but to learn to ride fear free.

Helmet. Also consider purchasing and wearing a helmet. Opinions on helmets vary, and as an adult, it is your right to choose whether or not to wear one, but consider this: few other items can so easily make a difference in the fear-free journey, and a helmet is one tool that can immediately make you feel more confident and help you stay safe. Why not use it?

Breed of Horse. Do you naturally gravitate to one breed over another? Are there breeds that you dislike? If so, you are completely normal. Everyone in the horse world has breed preferences, but there are also many misconceptions about breed characteristics based on exaggerated or untrue ideas. Remember that these are stereotypes, and while many may be based on some grain of truth, they do not reflect accurately on all members of the breed. Be willing to let go of your breed prejudices, and you may find that a "crazy, uncontrollable" Arab or "stubborn" Appaloosa is the perfect horse to help you become fear free.

Dealing with a Teacher's Bias. Teachers can have biases too, and you need to be aware of them. Some resist helmet use, believing it projects novice or inexperience, and some think that fear comes only from a lack of knowledge, believing that education alone will work. Some teachers may think a rider who chooses not to wear a helmet is reckless and unsafe; it is, however, their choice as adults. Some riding instructors and trainers simply do not believe that fearful people have any business handling horses or riding them at all. And if you discover a teacher who either does not respect your choice to protect yourself or who believes fearful riders are a "lost cause," then it is *not* your job to change his mind. Move on to a teacher who accepts and respects you, who sees the strength required for you to seek help, and who views healthy fear as common sense in disguise rather than a weakness.

> if you discover a teacher who believes fearful riders are a "lost cause," then it is not your job to change their mind. Move on to someone else.

Feeling Fear and Releasing Emotions

It is important never to feel fear while you are learning to ride fear free. Feeling fear while riding reinforces the fear memories and does nothing to extinguish fear, and you are trying to create new, fear-free memories. But once you have developed a healthy ability to regulate your fear response, you may be asked to relive or recall your fearful memories in order to better disrupt or extinguish their power over you. (See chapter 2, "Disrupting Fear Memories.")

During this part of the process, you will still never be asked to put yourself in danger or to do anything you are not comfortable doing. In fact, to begin, you will be away from your horse. And later, after you have learned to experience the memory and release the fear it causes, you'll be able to do the same while riding.

This is one of the most difficult aspects of the journey to fear-free riding, but it is probably the most rewarding. By practicing techniques for dealing with lower levels of anxiety in a safe setting, you will learn ways to cope with higher levels of fear. In addition, your work with releasing all your emotions will help temper your reaction to any scary circumstance.

Taking Your Own Journey

One of the greatest temptations you will face is to compare yourself with someone else. There will always be someone who is a braver rider, who has more money, who rides a better trained horse, or who is a faster learner. You will also encounter riders who are less bold or slower learners, and you gain nothing by comparing yourself to them. It doesn't matter what someone else can do with her horse or even what someone else can do with your horse. What matters is what you feel comfortable doing with your horse.

The journey to being fear free is not a race. Don't waste your time by comparing yourself to other riders. Set your own pace and enjoy the ride.

Photo by Laura Daley.

Focusing on Your Successes. As you go through the process of becoming fear free, the what-ifs will always outweigh the positives. That sounds terribly bleak, but it is the truth. No matter how far you come or how much you progress, you will always be able to imagine situations that undermine your confidence. You can ride the horse at a walk in the arena, but what if he breaks into a trot? You can ride to the pond, but what if a duck flies in front of the horse as you go around it? This type of hypothetical speculation has no limit. You will always be able to conjure up a negative to cancel out the positives you have achieved.

This is why it is imperative to focus on your successes and try to transform what-if thinking into preparation. For example, if you find yourself asking what if, then build on your success by thinking of what specific thing you have learned to do that would help you deal with your what-if situation. What techniques have you learned to deal with the hypothetical scary event?

Remembering your successes and applying those lessons to future rides will help you on your journey.

Seeing the Small Steps That Lead to the Big Goal. As a fearful rider, you will always be so focused on accomplishing the thing that scares you most that you will not be able to see all the steps that will help get you there without fear.

In fact, this focus on completing the physical task is one of the main problems with traditional approaches to dealing with riding fear. Both the rider and the teacher are focused on the wrong thing: achieving the riding goal. But the real goal is riding fear free. Focusing on the riding task may or may not result in your being able to do that specific thing. But focusing on learning to ride fear free means that you will have the tools and skills to achieve *any* riding goal, not just the one that scares you the most right now.

For example, let's say your goal is to trail ride, and you are having your first lesson on the trail. You are likely envisioning your "ideal trail ride." You see yourself mounting up and riding for ten miles across all kinds of terrain. You go right to the riding goal, and you likely begin to feel anxiety.

So you cannot start with the riding goal. Remember the real goal is not trail riding; it is trail riding *fear free*. You must start where you feel no fear. Where do you feel no fear? Can you get on and off the horse without feeling fear? Can you ride two steps without fear? Can you ride to that tree and back without fear? Can you ride to the next tree and back without fear? As you begin to do the small steps, you will see how they add up to meeting both your specific riding goal and your general goal of riding fear free.

Dealing with Change

Sometimes fear of the unknown, even after great progress, can be a stumbling block in your journey. The loss of a horse, problems at home, a big move, the loss of a loved one, children moving out (or maybe moving back in), or a change of barns can temporarily arrest your progress.

If struggles with life issues outside the horse arena are negatively affecting your riding progress, there is nothing wrong with going back to an easier step in the lesson. Find one thing that you do completely fear free, and repeat and perfect it. Do not try to learn a new task or take on a new fear in the midst of big life changes. Your progress comes from within yourself and is not dependent on your horse, trainer, barn, or discipline. When you believe it comes from within yourself, you will be truly fear free with any horse at any time doing any task at any place regardless of external circumstances.

Finally Riding Fear Free

You are in charge of your destiny, and by understanding the nature of fear and doing the hard work to extinguish it, you have given yourself the chance at riding fear free. But the concepts of memory replacement and your new ability to see reality and react accordingly can positively affect the rest of your life. You will not only *ride* fear free but will also *live* fear free.

Notes

Twelve

Helping Riders Become Fear Free: A Teacher's Perspective

Photo by Jim Bush.

A professional who has gone through specific accredited training has an advantage in making the transition to helping fearful students, but any teacher can help a fearful rider. The most important virtue of a fear-free facilitator is that she is willing to become a teacher of students rather than merely remaining an instructor. It may seem like semantics, but words are meaningful. A teacher guides and tries to bring the student along at his or her own pace, while an instructor lays out the lesson and tells the pupil how to get there. An instructor never allows the student's needs to dictate the lesson but coaches, drills, and practices until the goal is achieved.

As a riding instructor or trainer, you are not required to take on fearful riders as students if that is not truly what you want to do. Not all teachers want to delve into this area, and that's okay. Be honest about your interests, and then relay the truth to the prospective student.

If you agree to help fearful students, then your job is to let go of your biases and start to help them overcome and replace their fear memories. If you are a horse trainer, you will likely be tempted to offer a horse-training solution—if you can just get the horse's body under control, then the rider will gain confidence. If you are a riding instructor, you might be tempted to offer a riding-technique solution—if you can just get the rider balanced, he will feel less

> As a riding instructor or trainer, you are not required to take on fearful riders as students if that is not truly what you want to do, but if you agree to help such a person, then your job is to let go of your biases and help the student replace her fear memories.

unstable and therefore more confident. But riding and training must be secondary to the rider's emotions and brain function.

The good news is that, as an experienced horse trainer and/or riding instructor, you already understand that small steps are needed to reach the end goal, and you have the basic understanding of what you need to do to help a fearful rider.

Correcting Misconceptions about Fearful Riders

Instructors can be the positive catalyst that starts fearful riders on their journey. As confident riders, teachers often need to reevaluate their notions of fearful riders. If you have never had to deal with one or if you have never had to overcome a riding fear yourself, you may not have a realistic understanding of what it takes for someone to admit that she is fearful and needs help.

Examine your preconceived ideas and biases. Before you can truly help fearful students, you must have a good understanding of what they are and what they are not.

Misconceptions about Fearful Riders

Is fear a lack of knowledge or riding skill?

If fear comes from a lack of education, then a knowledgeable horseman never needs to be afraid. But there are actually many reasons a highly educated, well-trained horseperson may become afraid. In fact, the more educated someone is, the more he knows to fear. Therefore, fear can actually be worse for a highly educated person.

Some fearful students *do* need to learn horsemanship skills, but the majority of them have already tried to overcome their fears by studying and practicing basic riding and training techniques. They have attended expos and clinics, purchased training DVDs, had their horses trained by professionals, and taken hours—if not years—of lessons. So when these riders finally admit their fear and that they cannot progress further without addressing it, know that their fear does not come from lack of study. They are educated horsepeople, and they are looking to you, their teacher, to help find the missing link in their riding journey.

Do timid or fearful people have any business trying to handle or ride a horse?

This question assumes that timid or fearful people cannot learn to overcome their fears or act assertively, and that premise is patently untrue. Any fear can be overcome. But in order to overcome a fear of horses, people have to learn how to interact with them in a safe environment, and that is why they come to you in the first place. If you choose to work with fearful riders, then your job is to teach them to overcome fear in the safest environment with the safest horses you can provide, just as you would with a young child or beginning rider. If your student is brave enough to seek help, then he or she is brave enough to ride a horse.

Does wearing a helmet mean the rider does not trust herself or her horse?

All adults have the right to choose whether or not they (or their children) will wear protective helmets. As a teacher and mentor, you should respect that choice, even if you disagree or view a helmet as a sign of weakness or a poor fashion choice. Wearing a helmet is actually a sign that the student understands how easily the brain can be damaged in a fall. After all, bicyclists wear helmets. Does that mean they don't trust their bikes to keep them safe? Of course not. By choosing to wear a helmet, the student demonstrates preparedness, and prepared, thinking riders are able to handle an emergency better than fearless riders who will be surprised when the unexpected happens.

And just as it is okay if students choose to wear a helmet, it is equally permissible for them to choose not to wear one. Not wearing a helmet does not mean riders are reckless or out of control. As long as they understand the potential consequences of riding without a helmet and sign a helmet liability release, you need to respect their choice. If this is against your barn policy, you may have to refuse service, but why not consider offering them the chance to learn about the wise use of helmets by seeing the examples set by your other students?

But they look so relaxed and in control. How can they be fearful?

Many fearful riders appear relaxed and competent in the saddle, but inside they are screaming in fear. Some are naturally good riders, but many of them have spent years with riding instructors and trainers hoping that improvement of their skill or the horse's behavior will eliminate their fear. They have already exhausted most riding and training solutions, and they need you to remember that the physical tasks are secondary to training their brains to ride fear free.

Empathizing with a Student's Fear

As a horse professional, it is likely that you have never experienced the level of fear or the type of anxiety your students face; therefore, you will need to use your imagination and show empathy when working with them. When a student comes to you for help with his fear, your first priority should be to understand which fear level—broken confidence, functioning fear, non-functioning fear, repressed fear, or irrational fear—he fits as described in chapter 1. While you will use the same techniques no matter what level he fits, knowing exactly what you are dealing with will help you better understand and empathize with the student.

Origins of Rider Fear: Do They Matter? Many articles and books that deal with rider fear begin by listing reasons people become afraid of horses. Some people are involved in riding accidents, and some just witness them. Some people become fearful as they age and their bodies don't bounce as easily as they used to. Some are naturally more timid.

While knowing the root of a rider's fear may prove helpful on her journey to fear free, especially if she is dealing with a major accident, it is not critical. You can use the techniques in this book to develop lesson plans for any fearful rider at any stage in his or her journey. No matter where the fear originates, the same techniques are used.

Sometimes knowing the specific nature of a rider's worst fears can help an instructor, but it is not a good idea to grill a student on this subject. Many riders have worked to repress or hide their fear and may not actually know its cause, so it is impossible for them to explain why they are afraid. Other students are so traumatized that having to relive the experience is actually counterproductive and harmful to the process. First, reduce their fear with fear-free techniques before trying to get them to relive the trauma.

Rather than forcing a student to verbalize trauma, keep in mind the five basic fears that all humans face: death, mutilation or injury, loss of autonomy or entrapment, separation, and ego-death (Albrecht, "Five Basic Fears"). The fear of death and injury can easily be applied in a riding context, but what about the others? Loss of autonomy might manifest itself as fear of losing control of the horse or freezing in the saddle, and fear of separation could be seen as fear of rejection by barn friends, trainers, or riding instructors or even of standing out in a crowd. Ego-death is fear of failure or humiliation, feeling stupid, or disappointing oneself. All of these fears are handled with the principles outlined in *Riding Fear Free*, but by knowing your riders' likely fears, you can address them by bringing up imaginary scenarios and their successful conclusions.

For example, if you choose to address the fear of failure, you might ask your students to talk or write about the worst that might happen if they fail. Let them describe their feelings in detail, or, if they have no idea, it is your turn to give an example of failure and its results. You might talk about how you failed to follow traffic laws by breaking the speed limit on the way to the barn. You did not follow the letter of the law, so you are not perfect, and in reality, you fail all the time.

Then, go one step further. If you are trying to learn something new, do you expect to do it right the first time? Of course not. So doing something wrong (failure) is actually part of learning how to do it right. Failure can help someone improve and excel. When you take this lesson back to the ring and apply it to failing as a rider, you will be able to show students how mistakes fit into the learning curve and how failure makes them better riders and horse handlers.

Even if you cannot sympathize with riders' fears, you can choose to be vulnerable and show that you are not as perfect as they imagine. Relate a story of a difficult lesson or ride—but *not* a traumatic event—to show that even you had to overcome something. Lead by example. If you expect your students to be honest, you should be honest first. If you want students to be carefree and have fun, that attitude must start with you.

Understanding the Teacher's Role: You Are Not in Charge

This may sound shocking, but when it comes to learning to overcome fear, the rider is always in control of the lesson. When a student enters your barn and tells you that she is afraid, you should immediately adjust your priorities and goals accordingly. You are no longer primarily a riding instructor or trainer; you are an emotional supporter. Your goal is not to get the student to do a task physically; your goal should be for her to be emotionally fear free when she undertakes the physical task.

> The student is always in charge of the lesson.

If the rider begins to exhibit fear or asks to stop or slow down, then it is important that you immediately adjust your lesson plan. It is your job to help the fearful rider recognize his fear and then help him let it go. If you do not stop the moment a fearful student asks you to stop, you are teaching him to suppress and ignore his fear, not release it for good.

As a teacher, you are an emotional supporter as a student works through the difficult tasks on her journey to riding fear free. Your role is more of a guide, helping students see their small successes and guiding them to return to easier sections of a lesson plan if they get stuck or afraid. Sometimes, no amount of riding and practice will help certain fearful students. If a rider's fear is debilitating or more than you think you should handle, consider encouraging her to seek professional help from a licensed doctor. Also, if a seemingly normal student dredges up repressed or forgotten painful memories, encourage him to seek immediate care from a licensed, professional counselor. Do not present yourself as anything more than the professional teacher and horseperson that you are.

Developing a Lesson Plan

Help your students write a lesson plan, especially if you are new at helping fearful riders. Physically sitting down and writing a step-by-step plan is one of the best things you can do to ensure that both you and your student are on the same page and that no one is surprised by what follows. This is not something that should be done in the middle of the ring as the student enters; you should consider it carefully in a quiet place.

This activity will help develop a rider's trust in you and allow her to begin opening up and letting go of her fears. It will also remind you not to push the student or treat her like every other student you teach. It will help you remember that she is dealing with personal issues that make her feel vulnerable, and a written lesson plan will force you both to see and celebrate every small success.

Understanding the Learning Curve

As with all other types of instruction or study, fearful riders will experience a learning curve while overcoming their fear. The more they practice riding without fear, the easier it will become. As they progress along the curve, they will make mistakes, and their performance may go from good to bad to better to worse before they finally learn to ride fear free. Teachers need to give students time and freedom to make mistakes and learn from them.

> Mistakes are a necessary part of the learning process. Until you make mistakes, you cannot truly learn.

Teachers have several options for helping their students through mistakes while on the learning curve. When your student seems to make the same error repeatedly, stop and laugh about it, make it funny, or do some bad or incorrect movements of your own. Show him that it is no big deal if he does it more than a few times. Or consider taking a water break. Drink a quick sip and move on. But the best option is to return to a simpler step in the lesson and perfect it before going back to the more difficult exercise. Often, the student will then be able to perform the "difficult" task easily and without thought. If the end of your lesson time is approaching and the student still struggles, then work on the previous step in the lesson to finish your time together. It is always best to leave the student wanting more and not fighting to learn something.

Fielding Questions

Some riders become fearful when they stop questioning their situation and the reasons for doing what they do. They have begun blindly accepting lessons without asking why they are doing them or if they are ready to take the next step. As a result, students may push through their fear just to please the teacher, and because they do not truly understand why an exercise works, they may not be invested in the lesson. As a teacher, you should encourage your students to ask questions and be prepared to answer them so that both their conscious thoughts and their subconscious emotions will be actively engaged in the process.

However, some students use questions to deflect or delay the lesson. If you have already thoroughly explained the reasons you are asking them to do something, then their persistent questions may actually indicate fear. In these cases, consider asking the students to write their questions in their journal entry for the lesson so that you can answer them later. But in addition, adjust your lesson plan so that you are not pushing students to the point of fear.

Using Positive Reinforcement

Experienced teachers already know the value of praise, compliments, and positive reinforcement in their lesson programs. These tools are also vital in helping fearful riders believe in themselves enough to open up and change long-standing beliefs and habits. Teachers should look for the slightest change in students' attitudes and behaviors, and praise them for their effort.

If you give a compliment and the rider corrects you or tries to deflect it, then he has not totally committed to the exercise or is still experiencing some form of fear or doubt. One of the most difficult aspects of helping fearful riders is convincing them of their own progress and self-worth. Your positive reinforcement will help them realize that they are good riders and that their fear issues are resolving.

When you pay a compliment, listen for code words to decide whether your rider accepts her progress or if she still has doubts. The phrase "Yeah, but…" is a major clue that riders still have some fear to process. When they hear a compliment that they do not feel worthy of, teach them to say, "I can accept that." This positive response will help them get comfortable with the idea or compliment without rejecting it altogether.

Appropriate physical touch can help fearful riders ease tension and provide positive reinforcement of their success. The teacher becomes a natural ground for them, and a handshake, pat on the back, or high five changes their mental state immediately. Start slowly because some fearful people do not like sudden touches, but most people will not refuse a quick handshake or high five.

Rewarding Your Students

Recognizing and rewarding your students for taking risks and accomplishing their goals is an important aspect of a successful lesson program. Much like positive reinforcement and verbal praise, physical rewards help students see and understand their own successes.

Consider giving out certificates for bravery or completion of a lesson, and use small candies, stickers, or toys as rewards even for adult students. But don't use rewards in the traditional way—when a student accomplishes a physical task. Instead, focus on attitude and thoughts. If your normally negative student says something even remotely positive, reward him. Or when your quiet, reserved, and proper student finally tries to do something out of her comfort zone like look silly or celebrate, give her a reward and celebrate as if she just won first place in a big show. For that student, being positive or celebrating a success *is* a huge moment in her journey to fear free.

Directing a Spook

Have you ever watched a horse start to pull away from its handler? Usually, the handler's reaction is to jerk on the rein and shout "whoa!" as the horse drags him halfway across the parking lot. The handler's resistant reaction usually scares the horse more and sends him into high-flight mode so that he is now running from the handler as well as the initial spook. What would have happened if the handler had kept tension on the rein but continued to walk with the horse, going with his fight instinct instead of trying so hard to shut it down? By following the momentum of the horse but keeping pressure on the rein or lead, you allow his flight instinct to diminish naturally rather than trying to force him to stop, which often makes the flight worse. Once his flight instinct diminishes and he is thinking again, he will give to the pressure on the rein, and the handler will have worked both the horse's mind by allowing him to come down from his spook naturally and his physical training by keeping pressure on the rein and releasing only when the horse has offered the correct response.

The same applies to fearful riders in the middle of a spook. Go with their fears and even make them seem bigger than they imagine. This is usually accomplished with words and not by physically making a spook so big that someone gets hurt or the rider panics. Keep talking until the verbal scenario is so overblown and out of proportion to reality that the student has to stop and take stock of the true situation. Once he stops and asks good questions about what is truly happening, he will see that reality was not as big as his fears led him to believe.

As the teacher, when you see tension building, instead of waiting for it to burst, do a little spook by giving a gentle startle: say boo to the rider or blow a raspberry to jolt the horse. This will bring the horse and rider back into the here and now. When they startle, help them to laugh it off and explain that they worked through their emotions in a controlled environment. Neither the horse nor rider got so scared that the incident became counterproductive to the lesson.

Teach your students to do the same when they feel their horses starting to get excited or emotional. As they sense the horses' emotions starting to rise, encourage them to give a little jolt or raspberry to help the animals release tension in a controlled way. The riders know the spook is coming, and it will be small compared to what it could have been. It will be a spook in place, not a bolt, and riders can praise their horses for calming down. Encourage them to laugh, say "just kidding" to the horses, or ask them if they are feeling better now. Saying the words aloud helps settle handlers and their horses. This helps riders release their own pent-up tension.

Directing a startle will immediately return power to the riders, who have now developed a way to diffuse a spook before it gets out of control. And whether or not they understand it, fearful riders can sense when their horses are in the beginning stages of a spook. Once they have tried directing a few spooks, their whole attitude toward riding will change.

Making the Situation Easier

When a student struggles in a traditional lesson, the teacher naturally pushes her to improve by more practice, better examples to follow, or more drills. In other words, the teacher keeps the pressure on the student until she has completed that section of the learning curve. But when a fearful person struggles, the best thing to do is stop and return to an easier part of the lesson plan.

Reviewing the previous step is not failure; instead, it is perfecting the basics in order to excel. Professional athletes spend most of their practice time working on the fundamentals of their sport. They are always reviewing the basics. If that is the best way for million-dollar athletes to hone their skills, why is it not best for riding students? The more adept they become at the basics of each exercise, the more quickly they master the difficult maneuvers and the sooner they ride fear free.

> When a fearful person is struggling, the best thing to do is stop and return to an easier part of the lesson plan.

Being Patient

Fearful riders are already at the edge of their emotional capacity, and working with them effectively requires a patient teacher. By the time they actually seek help for their fears, they are usually so over the top that any note of disapproval from the teacher could send them crashing down. Therefore, you should try not to get frustrated around fearful riders; they need you to be their rock. Because they are already too hard on themselves, they need you to be understanding as you guide them through this process. You must maintain a positive, upbeat attitude and find the good in their every effort.

A patient teacher can put fear into perspective, making it smaller.

Never Saying I Told You So

If a student is having a great day, and he exclaims, "I *am* a good rider," then don't say, "I told you so." Instead, join in his newfound confidence by agreeing and telling him how amazing he is. After building a solid rapport and hearing him make other positive statements about his ability, you may be able to tease him and start asking if he is ready to believe you the first time you say something. But some students never appreciate an "I told you so," no matter how well meaning it is, so if you choose to tease them, keep it to a minimum. Fearful riders already deal with enough negative emotions and do not need teasing to undermine their progress. Praise is always a good choice in lieu of saying, "I told you so."

Making a Correction Sandwich

Teachers do need to correct fearful students, and the best way to correct anyone, especially a fearful student, is by making a correction sandwich. First, praise or compliment the student on something she has done right. Second, make the correction. Third, immediately follow the correction with another statement of praise. Because the correction is sandwiched between two statements of true praise, it is far easier to accept than a correction alone.

> **The Correction Sandwich**
> (1) Praise or compliment the student on something they have done right.
> (2) Make the correction.
> (3) Immediately follow the correction with another statement of praise.

Taking Breaks

After a great "light-bulb" moment or when the student has experienced a fear jolt, take a break. This pause gives the mind a chance to catch up with what is going on physically, and it also keeps riders from feeling pressured. They learn that it is perfectly acceptable and encouraged to stop, step back, and relax. The goal is to stop the focus on the lesson and put it onto something so easy that riders do not have to think about it.

Leading Questions

Teachers can help lessen a rider's anxiety level by asking leading questions, especially if tempted to help the rider along with a little push. Verbalize your thoughts to get the rider to believe that you are going to ask him to do "the scary thing." If he fears jumping, then, as he rides around the arena, ask if he is ready to jump. Then, with a slight laugh, tell him he will not be jumping today. Instead, you have a whole lesson plan to go through first. These types of questions raise a fearful rider's emotions, but they do not actually push him into jumping early.

Before a rider can jump without fear, she must first be able to think about jumping without anxiety. That is why you talk about the frightening activity while she does something easy and fun, and then get her mind completely off it again. For that brief moment, she thinks she is really going to jump, but then you take the option away. This raises her anxiety, but by doing something easy instead, she experiences a little fear and can immediately control it.

My Student Is Not Progressing

If you find yourself or your student stuck, take inventory by asking good questions about what is happening in the lessons. Are you following the written lesson plan? Is the student engaging and committed to the exercise? Does he need to go to an easier section in the lesson, or does he need a challenge by adding speed or repetitions?

As a teacher, you may need to do a self-check. Are you doing or saying anything that your student could take as pressure? Could your jokes be undermining her success? Are you being positive and celebrating every small success? Are you working a step-by-step lesson plan, or did you think that she is riding so well that it would not hurt to skip a few steps?

Overriding Is *Not* the Answer

This sounds counter-intuitive, but too much physical riding can hinder the process of becoming fear free. Most fearful people have already worked hard to become technically correct riders. If hours of physical practice alone could have made them fear free, then

Photo by Laura Daley.

they would have already attained the goal. Hour upon hour of drilling or pattern memorization is not helpful because the startling truth is that most of the work to become fear free happens *off the horse*. As fearful people actively ride, they have to deal with stimuli, perform physical actions, and stay present with the horse at all times. They don't fully process what has happened until they are somewhere quiet and can review or write about what they experienced. Once away from the horse, the subconscious has a chance to process the ride and store the new, positive memories. Allowing students time to be still and marinate in what they've just done will allow their brains to catch up and replace bad memories with the good ones you both spent an hour creating.

Not Pushing the Student...

As a teacher and emotional supporter, never ask students to do more than they are capable of giving freely. No matter how confident you are in the horse's training or the rider's ability to perform a task, it is never a good idea for a teacher to push the rider into doing anything for which she is not emotionally prepared. However, it is your job to push riders to *see their progress, to see the reality of the situation, to accept compliments, and to believe they have changed and are fear free*.

Rather than focusing on the goal, try to make each lesson a series of questions and suggestions as you prepare riders to make the decision to undertake the task themselves. Fearful riders must be in control of every activity because only they can determine when something raises their anxiety or fear. It is also vital, however, for the teacher to help students recognize their fear responses on their own.

Asking questions will help both teachers and students clarify the fear issues that prevent them from performing the task without fear.

Both the teacher and the student must agree that at no point in the lesson should the student feel pressured into doing anything. This does not mean the teacher cannot raise the student's emotions at various points throughout the lesson. For example, while the student is working at the walk, the teacher may throw out a suggestion to lope. If the student agrees to try, ask him to do a fear check. Ask him to determine for himself if loping is the wisest thing to do. The student's emotions are raised just by thinking about loping, but then you bring him back to reality and, instead of letting him lope, you do something fun or silly to change his state of mind. This pushes the student not to lope but to examine his emotions and circumstances and then make the decision to lope on his own.

Photo by Jin Bush.

...But Encouraging Them to the Next Level

Only experience can develop the feel and timing for instructing a fearful rider, just as it takes time to learn the techniques of horse training. It can be difficult to know when to suggest—not push—moving to the next level or when to back off. However, the beautiful thing about this conundrum is that if you make a mistake and the rider actually feels fear when you suggest going to the next level, then you can treat it like a "just kidding" moment as described in "Leading Questions."

This will change your "mistake" into an opportunity to get the student's emotions working and then release the pressure. You may recognize it as a mistake, but the student only sees the same pattern you have used all along—approach and retreat—and lets go of the fear that much faster.

In an ideal situation, the student would do all the suggesting. She would tell you she is bored and wants to try something new. But sometimes the teacher has to take initiative. Since these lessons are about emotional control, then the teacher needs to observe even the slightest body language from the student. A great instructor will recognize the body language of fear before the rider does and move to control it.

Allowing a rider—either consciously through suggestions or subconsciously through body language—to direct a lesson goes against everything traditional instructors are taught when first learning to give riding lessons. In a traditional lesson, when a student resists, we push, cajole, or outright tell him to buck up and do it. Riders reluctantly do what they are told, and afterward, they usually grin and say how fun it was. This works because confident students are engaged and generally balanced in their emotions. Or perhaps they only needed one positive experience to forget their fear, and overall, the exercise is stored in the brain as a good thing. On the other hand, some riders learn to suppress their fear but grin outwardly at the physical accomplishment of the task. Pay attention to all your students and make sure you are not creating more riders who repress their fear.

Special Considerations for Teachers

Keeping Notes on Each Student. Track the progress of your students after each lesson. By updating a binder or information sheet, you will be able to see holes in their lessons and record their journey to riding fear free from your own perspective. After the riders are fear free, you can use your notes to show them how far they have come. This is especially good for young riders who cannot write well yet or for students who do not keep a journal for other reasons. Your notes will also prevent you from pushing your students and can help you develop better lesson plans and spark your creativity. Be sure to keep old lesson plans, written assignments, drawings, notes, and rewards to show the students later.

Dealing with Changing Circumstances. Sometimes fear of the unknown, even after great progress, can stop students in their tracks. The loss of a horse, problems at home, or changing barns can arrest the progress of fearful riders.

Note changes in your students' circumstances and encourage them to challenge themselves if they are normally eager and then suddenly full of excuses. Make sure they understand that their progress does not come from their horse, trainer, barn, or discipline but from within themselves.

Teaching People-pleasing Perfectionists

People-pleasing perfectionists (PPPs) are the most difficult riders to teach. How can this be? PPPs are the most accommodating, hardest-working riders. If you ask for a journal entry, PPPs will come back with a novel with glossary, chapter titles, index, and highlighted sections for easy reading. They are the most accommodating, and that is the problem.

PPPs have been conditioned to deny themselves and put even total strangers first, so when an authority figure or someone they admire asks them to do something, they simply start performing. PPPs are so used to sacrificing self to win the approval of the person in charge that they have no gauge for their own emotions. They don't even consider their emotions.

PPPs are driven to complete the task or exercise perfectly, and they will go out of their way to please the instructor. They love lesson plans, goals, and step-by-step assignments. The teacher's job is to redefine success in the minds of PPPs; the goal is no longer to do a particular task but to engage their emotions. They will still perform a task in the lesson, and they will still probably work like crazy for your approval, but the real goal is to engage their emotions. Even if a student performs the exercise perfectly, you need to make her aware of her emotional state. If she has shut down, then your job is to point out that she is *failing* the lesson. Those are harsh words for PPPs, but they need to realize that their real goal has changed. They are not merely supposed to perform a task; they are to perform it fear free. Even more so than other types of fearful riders, PPPs need to approach a lesson from the perspective of emotions and not performance.

In order to best help PPPs, the teacher must encourage them to step back and stop viewing each lesson as an exercise that must be perfected in order to gain approval. Instead, they need to focus on tuning into their own emotions. When it comes to PPPs, the teacher will have to look, listen, and question every task to make sure they have not shut down their feelings and begun performing in order to please the teacher. These students must learn to engage and process every step.

One good way to introduce the concept of emotions over physical tasks to PPPs is to give them a job to do, but ask them to repeat the instructions to you before they begin the assignment. When they proudly repeat the physical assignment verbatim while omitting the emotional aspect completely, tell them that they have misunderstood the point of their fear-free riding lessons. The real point is to do those tasks without fear, so the first step in every lesson is for students to determine how they feel about that specific task.

> PPPs are so used to sacrificing themselves to win the approval of the person in charge that they have no gauge for their own emotions. They don't even consider their own emotions.

Because they did not stop to check their emotions, at this point they need to do something to change their state. Sing a silly song, do ups and downs, do jumping jacks, or do some other physical task to motivate them to check their hidden emotions before doing any assignment. Silly tasks are a huge motivator for PPPs because most do not like to be the center of attention or to do something silly. However, you are conditioning them to do a personal fear check before simply agreeing to do something for others.

To help PPPs examine their motives for their actions, it's good to ask "why" questions while they ride. The questions do not have to pertain to horses or the lesson but can address other portions of their lives. Ask why or what is their motivation behind doing something. Usually, they have never examined why they did things and just looked for the approval of the person asking for the task.

Perfectionists are always concerned about making a mistake or failing, so a change of thinking in this department is usually necessary. Remind them that mistakes do not mean defeat; they are only defeated when they stop trying. Mistakes are part of all people's learning processes, so in order to improve they must mess up. By trying to be perfect even while learning a new skill, PPPs may actually sabotage their overall success. Teachers must constantly remind PPPs of the learning curve and teach them to gauge where they are in the learning process. Encourage and celebrate mistakes because PPPs will never learn without them.

Have you ever helped people or prevented them from making a mistake and then been surprised by their angry response? What teachers sometimes fail to realize is that by "helping," perhaps they have taken away the student's opportunity to grow by learning her lesson herself. There is a lot of freedom in standing back and letting people make their own mistakes, so resist the temptation to prevent students from messing up unless they are putting themselves in danger. Allow them to make the mistake, but be there to praise them for trying and to help them along the rest of the learning curve. By "helping too much" or stopping someone from making a mistake, the teacher often hinders the learning process.

Praise and small tokens of appreciation go a long way with PPPs. Certificates of improvement and other rewards are great motivators, but make sure you reward their emotional effort and change in thinking rather than their physical actions.

Teaching Riders with Physical Limitations.

Whether a student is dealing with a lifetime physical limitation or something more recent, it is just one more step in the fear-free process. Even a lack of mobility or flexibility due to injury or the aging process can be scary for a fearful rider. Teachers and riders should work together to find ways to adjust their riding habits or expectations. Students must realize that they cannot change their physical limitations, so the sooner they accept the situation, the sooner they can deal with real problems. Everyone can see they might be missing a leg and make accommodations, but no one can see the fear that has kept them from their passion: horses. In the same way, many physically whole riders have something missing on the inside, and they go through life with a worse handicap than any physical limitation.

Helping Relatives

In general, it is a good idea to avoid trying to help your spouse or child ride fear free. Although it seems as if the intimacy of an existing relationship will make it easier for students to open up, such closeness can actually make honesty more difficult. The parent-child or marriage relationship can prevent students from revealing their innermost thoughts for fear of the consequences or judgment of their parent or partner. On the other side, teachers of relatives may feel more pressure to "solve the problem," and they may be more apt to take things personally during the process. Because people often treat strangers better and with more respect than relatives, it is usually best to let someone else help a loved one through their fear-free journey.

Teaching Men vs. Women

Culture has established different expectations for the ways that men and women deal with fear. When they face the same scary situation, the man will often appear angry, and the woman will usually display her fear through anxious behavior. Male riders are more apt to show their fear through aggression, violent words and actions, and risk taking, while female riders may act out their anxiety by nagging the horse or trying to micromanage his every behavior. Men may try harder than their female counterparts to distance themselves from fear by ignoring or refusing to acknowledge it (Barecca, "Women's Fears vs. Men's Fears"). Teachers should be aware of the differences in the way fear manifests itself in men and women and be prepared to deal with both.

Teaching Children

Not everyone chooses to teach children, and it can be challenging, but it is also very rewarding. Children can be more willing than adults to try new things, and they are not as conditioned to behave "properly," thus they are more willing to play with their horses. Conversely, children can be difficult to diagnose as fearful riders. Many aggressive, hard-riding children are actually trying to outrun or outride their fear. Help them learn to have fun without ignoring their ability to recognize and react to a dangerous situation. Teach children discernment and common sense without triggering fear. Consider the following tips if you teach children.

Avoiding Labels. Avoid the temptation to label children as fearful even if they have some riding fears or have had an accident. Instead, keep things positive and upbeat. Never discuss their fears or accidents in front of them, and avoid telling stories about accidents you've had or seen. When talking with parents about their children's difficulties, always have students leave the room or go out of earshot. The more you introduce the concept of fear in connection with riding, the more a child will understand and gravitate to it. Young children especially cannot separate real from imagined events, and they cannot differentiate talk from reality. So it's possible to introduce new fear memories into a child's brain even if the fear-inducing event never happened to that child.

Being Flexible. Lesson plans should never be so rigid that they cannot be adjusted on the spot to reach the fearful child where she is for that lesson. If the child seems fearful, do not hesitate to scrap the whole lesson and teach in the moment. Tell jokes as you lead the horse, or encourage the child to talk about his favorite video game, movie, or school subject. Have children talk about themselves and their dreams. This type of distraction is bad if you are trying to teach a specific skill, but it can be beneficial if you are focusing on fear.

Answering "Why" and "I Can't." Children often ask "why" and say "I can't" because they have learned to control or direct an adult with these phrases. They also use these words as a defense mechanism to avoid feeling fear. Children who say "I can't" need to learn that they can do what is asked of them. That may mean working with them twice as hard in order to prove it. However, teachers need to be careful to understand exactly what the child means. If he is trying to tell you that he does not understand or that he is afraid when he says "I can't" or asks "why," then immediately stop and adjust the lesson so that he does understand or is no longer afraid.

Photo by Jennifer Etheridge Bruce,

Take the time to help children understand that words have meanings. If they say "I can't" or "why" because they don't understand or are afraid, then they need to learn better words to communicate what is really happening inside. Teach them to say, "I don't understand," "I am afraid," or "I can't yet, but I am learning." By correctly labeling their emotions and thoughts, they have control in a positive and respectful way.

Keeping It Simple and Fun. Children need to do the exercises and techniques that apply to them, but if you tell them they have to do fifty ups and downs, they will probably groan, cry, and resist. But if you ask them to play a game of Simon Says or Mother May I, then it is fun to get on and off the horse. Challenge their creativity and ask them to try to find as many ways as possible to mount and dismount, never repeating a method. Encourage them to try skipping to the horse, getting on from their knees, using obstacles as mounting blocks, or sliding off the horse's rear. Children can always come up with new ways to mount and dismount, and they will have fun while repeating the up/down exercise.

Instead of just grooming a horse, children can use markers, glitter, or tempera paint to decorate the horse. Label body parts, or draw the bones and skeleton of the horse. Because you are not really trying to teach them how to groom but rather to be fear free while working around the horse, change it up and make it fun. Once they are comfortable working in close proximity to the horse, then you can take the time to teach a fearless rider how to groom a horse properly.

Riding Fear Free Says

Student says: My horse does not like repetition, or my horse got bored.

Riding Fear Free **says:** The rider does not want to take the time to learn the skill. She wants instant gratification, so she stops before the learning curve even starts. The truth is that a horse's whole life is about routine: breakfast at sunrise, turnout all day, lessons, then dinner. Repeat. Horses thrive on and learn through repetition. And so do people. Patterns and routine are what the horse counts on to stay calm in a stressful situation.

Student says: I can't.

Riding Fear Free **says:** This means that the teacher has discovered the rider's limit, and it's time to step back to something he can do and build from there. This is actually a good thing to hear because it means the student is willing to share his vulnerabilities and fears and is not just going to cowboy up. Encourage him to say, "I can't yet, but I'm learning."

Student says: Why?

Riding Fear Free **says**: Usually teachers hear this from children who are deflecting, but adults may use it to avoid their fears as well. Usually, this indicates that the rider is starting to experience some emotion, and it scares her so she tries to divert the instructor by asking questions. Be sure to explain why you are asking the rider to do something so that she will understand fully and thus commit fully, but if it becomes clear that she understands and is using questions to avoid fear, then redirect her back to the lesson, but find an easier step that will help the student accept the lesson without fear.

Student says: Yeah, but....

Riding Fear Free **says:** The student is either trying to cover up fear by protesting or is likely not listening to the teacher. Many fearful riders become defensive and have a comeback to your statements before they even engage in an activity or exercise. They want to pre-explain why they will fail. With a "yeah, but" student, teachers must engage their brains and bypass their mouths. Some are so used to challenging authority that they do not even know they are doing it.

Student says: My horse is not trained to do that, or my horse breed cannot do that.

Riding Fear Free **says:** The draft horse riders use for jousting *can* learn to chase a cow, jump cavaletti, or trail ride. A champion dressage horse *can* be a great trail companion or cattle sorting/penning steed on Friday nights. Will he win the world cutting championships? No, probably not, but cross-training is an important tool for all athletes. Change can greatly benefit the mental health and well-being of both horse and rider.

Student says: I can only ride my horse or do my discipline.

Riding Fear Free **says:** By riding other horses or trying other disciplines, riders will be able to raise and lower their fears in a controlled environment. Each time they have to adjust their thinking or riding, they are learning how to adjust during an emergency and to condition themselves not to freeze.

Student says: I have tried this exercise, and it did not work for me.

Riding Fear Free **says:** Chances are high that this student does not understand the point of the exercise, does not believe that it can help, or is simply not invested in the program. The teacher should explain the lesson and why it works, and then the student must agree to try to work the lesson until he is no longer just performing a task.

Notes

Thirteen

On the Other Side

Photo by Laura Daley.

When you understand and apply the techniques in this book, one day you will wake up to discover that you are a fear-free rider. Asking good questions will diminish your what-if thoughts, and you will see the reality of your situation more clearly than ever before. Raising and lowering your emotions will help ensure that you no longer overreact to any challenge you encounter with your horse. Your good memories will continue to grow, and your fearful memories will no longer have power over you.

> Learning to ride fear free will help you gallop joyously toward your dreams.

You will be fear free.

What Does This Mean for Me?

Will I ever experience fear again? Yes. And this is a *good* thing. Remember that the goal of this book is to help you learn to control your fear and to keep your fear from controlling you. You have learned techniques for managing your fear, but you cannot completely remove it from your life. And you shouldn't want to.

Fearlessness sounds like a good trait, but healthy fear keeps you from entering into situations that could hurt you, and it physically prepares you to react if you do end up in dangerous conditions. Healthy fear makes you faster and stronger; unhealthy fear causes panic and makes you unable to act. Being fear free means that you have learned to keep your fear in proportion to what is happening and to react in positive ways.

I know how to ask good questions. Will I ever have another horse-related accident? Unfortunately, accidents will happen. Being fear free does not exempt you from adhering to Newton's laws of physics. Gravity will always be there. What goes up must come down, and sometimes it comes down quite unexpectedly.

Accidents happen. It's an unavoidable fact of working with horses. According to Webster, an accident is "an unforeseen and unplanned event or circumstance." Even if you are a horse-reading savant or the world's greatest rider, you cannot anticipate every eventuality that may befall you. You can't accurately predict your horse's behavior or response to stimuli 100 percent of the time.

Even if you do see a wreck in the making, you may not choose the best way of dealing with it. Though you have learned to ask good questions to prevent you from getting yourself into a dangerous position, that doesn't mean you will never make a mistake. You aren't perfect. Your horse isn't perfect. As unsettling as it sounds, accidents are unavoidable.

> Using the techniques you learned in *Riding Fear Free*, you and your horse can overcome any obstacle.

Photo by Laura Daley

If I have an accident, will I go back to being as fearful as I was before? It is natural for formerly fearful riders to be afraid of being afraid. That sounds odd, but it is true. No one enjoys the feeling of fear, and no one wants to go back to the beginning of the fear journey and do it all again. The beauty of fear-free riding is that the exercises you've learned aren't necessarily designed for step-by-step use. You can pluck out the techniques you want and use them whenever you need them. You aren't going back to the beginning of anything; you are just going to have to pull out the techniques a little more often.

The exercises in this book work for dealing with both rational (experience-based) fear and irrational (what-if) fear. Even though the two types of fear are treated the same way, there is a difference between them. Rational fears are based on reality; you have experienced an accident or been hurt. Your resulting fear is completely valid. Irrational fears usually occur because riders are having trouble seeing the reality of their situation; you may not have had an accident, but your fear is still just as valid. And both types of fear are handled the same way.

Asking good questions, raising and lowering emotions, and creating good memories work for both types of fear. After an accident, you have a legitimate reason to be afraid, but you can still be fear free. You can still use these techniques to keep your fear from controlling you. It is possible to use the techniques in this book—along with any necessary changes in training—to overcome the effects of an accident.

Go back to where you feel no fear and continue the process of asking questions, raising and lowering emotions, and creating good memories, and you will soon see that the work you did before the accident of learning to control your emotions has indeed carried over post-trauma. You haven't lost your fear-free status at all; in fact, you have the opportunity to reinforce it further by practicing the techniques again. Think of it as the ultimate in raising and lowering the emotions. Your accident raised them, you will use exercises to lower them, and, ultimately, you will have even more control over them.

The only way that fear will control you again after an accident is if you do not continue using fear-free methods—those in this book and your personal stress-reducing techniques and support systems. You are in control of your fear-free status!

I am now a fear-free rider, but I don't know what to do next. You spent days, weeks, months, and years trying to overcome your fear. You focused on that issue, and suddenly you realize you are no longer paralyzed. You have freed yourself to try anything, do anything. But what now? It seems like you would just hop on your horse and ride off into the sunset with a smile on your face, but after being so focused for so long, you might actually feel at a loss. You may wonder why you did all that work if riding is still not truly fun.

The only way that fear will control you again after an accident is if you do not continue using fear-free methods—those in this book and your personal stress-reducing techniques and support systems. You are in control of your fear-free status!

Savor every moment with your horse as you continue on your fear-free journey.

Horses should never be a source of angst or stress, but formerly fearful riders may have forgotten why they started riding in the first place. Stop and take stock of your reasons for being involved with horses. Did you want to win blue ribbons at shows? Did you want to win barrel races or cut cattle? Or did you just want a relationship with such a majestic, noble creature? No matter what your reasons were for becoming involved with horses, you can rediscover the joy and magic that initially drew you. As you begin to pursue your goal—whether showing or trail riding—remember the simple things. When you rediscover joy in the small moments with your horse, you will begin having fun with him again, and you will be able to rekindle and build on your relationship with him, no matter how fear has strained it.

When was the last time you went to the barn to enjoy your horse's company? Do you always have a training or riding purpose in mind? Do you ever have a grooming day with your horse? Or just watch him graze in the pasture? Owning a horse does not mean that you have to ride every time you go to the barn. In fact, you don't ever have to ride. You can have horses just for the pleasure they bring as you watch them graze in the pasture or walk among them. You may like brushing their manes and tails. And that is okay.

Many people experience guilt for not riding, believing the horse suffers from lack of attention or thinking that he's not getting the chance to live up to his potential. But ask good questions. Is the horse really suffering? Probably not. If he's got adequate turnout in a nice pasture with a good herd, he's actually living in horsey paradise. And the only potential he has to live up to is to make you—his owner—happy. If just caring for and loving your horse brings you satisfaction, then he has lived up to his highest calling already.

Savor every moment with your horse because you never know when it may be gone. Pushing yourself too hard or doing activities with your horse that you do not truly enjoy may leave you regretting the time you spend with him. You don't want to regret your attitude, temper, or treatment of your horse, especially when you can lose him in an instant. Horse owners often take for granted just how fragile horses are.

While you continue your fear-free journey to the show ring or the trailhead, remember to be still with your horse every now and then and appreciate him for the individual he is. Don't compare yourself or your horse to others. Every person and horse is an individual with special talents and traits. Let your horse show you how amazing and special he can be if you allow his personality to shine.

Can I help others become fear free too? Once you become free from fear in all aspects of your life, you will be tempted to try to help, fix, or advise almost everyone you meet; however, if they are not truly ready to let go of their fear, they will likely reject you and the simplicity of these exercises. If you really want to cause lasting change in your friends and fellow horsepeople, lead by example and wait for them to notice your peace and control. Soon, they will ask how you changed.

Living Fear Free

By taking the time and effort to become a fear-free rider, you have brought yourself a measure of balance and peace, and you will soon notice that other stressful areas of your life will become less overwhelming as well. The science and techniques described in Riding Fear Free are not limited to horses; these principles and ideas can have a positive effect on every other aspect of your life.

Working to overcome horseback riding fear has helped you learn the basics for overcoming any sort of fear or anxiety. By asking good questions, seeing the reality of your situation, raising and lowering your emotions, and creating fear-free memories, you have freed yourself to accomplish your dreams. You can write a novel, go skydiving, or even deal more effectively with your children. Just apply Riding Fear Free's core principles to any fear-inducing situation.

Becoming fear free is a lifelong process, and you now have the tools to capture your emotions and to make conscious choices about how to feel and express them. Your fear no longer holds you prisoner, and you are prepared to live more fully and enjoy your horses knowing that you are *Riding Fear Free*.

Photo by Jim Bush.

Now that you are using the techniques in *Riding Fear Free*, you and your horse are looking in the same direction, and together, you can overcome any obstacle as you prepare to gallop joyously toward your dreams.

Bibliography

Albrecht, Kenneth. "The (Only) Five Basic Fears We All Live By." *Psychology Today*. 22 March 2012. http://www.psychologytoday.com/blog/brainsnacks/201203/the-only-five-basic-fears-we-all-live (accessed 26 April 2012).

Barecca, Gina. "Women's Fears vs. Men's Fears." Parts 1-3. *Psychology Today*. 20-30 September 2011. http://www.psychologytoday.com/blog/snow-white-doesnt-live-here-anymore/201109/are-womens-fears-different-mens-fears (accessed 8 May 2012).

Columbia Medical Center Newsroom. "Fleeting Images of Fearful Faces Show Where the Brain Processes Unconscious Anxiety, New Cumc Research." Columbia Medical Center. 17 December 2004. http://www.cumc.columbia.edu/news-room/2004/12/fleeting-images-of-fearful-faces-show-where-the-brain-processes-unconscious-anxiety-new-cumc-research-3/ (accessed 26 April 2012).

Horstman, Judith. *The Scientific American Day in the Life of Your Brain*. San Francisco: Jossey Bass, 2009.

Layton, Julia. "How Fear Works." *HowStuffWorks.com*. 13 September 2005. http://science.howstuffworks.com/environmental/life/human-biology/fear.htm (accessed 26 April 2012).

Lyons, John. *Fear in the Rider, Fear in the Horse*. Volume 3 of A Conversation with John Lyons. The Horse Show Audio Library. Lamb Stew Productions, 2003. 2 Compact Discs.

Öhman, Arne. "Fear and Anxiety as Emotional Phenomena: Clinical Phenomenology, Evolutionary Perspectives, and Information-Processing Mechanisms." *Handbook of Emotions*. Ed. Michael Lewis and Jeanette M. Haviland. New York: The Guilford Press, 1993.

Paul, Annie Murphey. "Your Brain on Fiction." *The New York Times Sunday Review*. 17 March 2012. http://www.nytimes.com/2012/03/18/opinion/sunday/the-neuroscience-of-your-brain-on-fiction.html?_r=2&pagewanted=all (accessed 7 May 2012).

Smith, James. "Emotional Control Circuit of Brain's Fear Response Discovered." *Medical News Today*. MediLexicon, Intl. 2 October 2006. http://www.medicalnewstoday.com/releases/53154.php (accessed 26 April 2012).

Society for Neuroscience, "Fear and Post-traumatic Stress Disorder." Society for Neuroscience. No date. http://www.sfn.org/index.aspx?pagename=publications_rd_fear_ptsd (accessed 26 April 2012).

Suzuki, Akinobu, Sheena A. Josselyn, Paul W. Frankland, Shoichi Masushige, Alcino J. Silva, and Satoshi Kida. "Memory Reconsolidation and Extinction Have Distinct Temporal and Biochemical Signatures." *The Journal of Neuroscience* 24/20 (19 May 2004). http://www.jneurosci.org/content/24/20/4787.full (accessed 26 April 2012).

Tamminga, Carol A. "The Anatomy of Fear Extinction." *The American Journal of Psychiatry* 163/6 (June 2006). http://ajp.psychiatryonline.org/article.aspx?Volume=163&page=961&journalID=13 (accessed 26 April 2012).

Other Resources

Goodnight, Julie. Julie Goodnight Natural Horse Training. http://www.juliegoodnight.com (accessed 14 May 2012).

Lyons, John. *Lyons on Horses*. New York: Skyhorse Publishing, 2009.

Meyners, Eckart. *Rider Fitness: Body and Brain: 180 Anytime, Anywhere Exercises to Enhance Range of Motion, Motor Control, Reaction Time, Flexibility, Balance and Muscle Memory in the Saddle.* North Pomfret VT: Trafalgar Square Books, 2011.

Shrake, Richard. *Western Horsemanship: The Complete Guide to Western Riding*. Fort Worth: Western Horseman, 2002.

Acknowledgements

Our deepest appreciation goes to everyone who helped make Riding Fear Free possible. Thank you to our editorial team: Marilyn Whiteley, Octavia Becton, and Kelley Fuller Land. Also, thank you, Dr. Beverle Graves Myers, for fact-checking our sections dealing with science and psychiatry. And to Jody Lyons goes our gratitude for sharing her story in the foreword.

We are also grateful to our artistic team, including illustrators Lydia Beccard and Jim Bush and photographers Bert Becton, Jennifer Etherton Bruce, Jim Bush (Jim and Emily Bush Fine Art Photography), Vicki Strickland (Vicki Strickland Photography), and Alicia VanderMeulen. Thank you to our models Johanna Fischer, Kymber Miller (BiSaddular), Ellyn Dickson, Stephanie Clegg (SC Equine), Jennifer Hooker, Vicki Strickland, Marie TeVelde, Henry TeVelde, Erin Hooker, Laura Hooker, Kaitlyn Dickson, Sarah Marcus, Emsley Bruce, Susan Calvin, Charlene Clegg, Sondra Marcus, and Katherine Strickland. Space constraints prevented the use of all the wonderful images captured at our photo shoots, but additional pictures will be featured on RidingFearFree.com in the future.

By Laura

I am grateful to my childhood and family experiences, which were not always easy but helped me become the woman I am today. A special thank-you to my father for giving me a positive outlook on life. He often said, "You can always wake up with a smile if you sleep with a coat hanger in your mouth." He always believed in me and had something positive to say. And I'm thankful that my mother instilled in me a desire to help animals and people. I know she would be proud that I finally put in print what she saw me do on a daily basis. I'm grateful that both my parents gave me a deep love of horses and the freedom to run wild and discover how to work around so many untamed and amazing animals. And a special thank-you to my big sister, who did the inside cooking and cleaning, leaving me free to be outside working and learning with the animals. If I had to do all the inside chores before heading outside, I never would have had time to play with the ponies.

I also would like to thank my students, therapeutic clients, friends, and lesson horses who trusted me enough to try my fear-free ideas. I would not have been able to develop my gifts without the help and trust of my students, clients, and friends. A special thanks to the Kjeldgaard family—Eric, Lisa, Nicholas, Stephen, Matt, Chris, Jack, Charlie, Kate and Grace—for helping me take my methods to the next level.

Finally, without Jennifer's belief in me and my methods, this book would never have been written. She has helped me grow and expand into a more rounded person by teaching me to write fear free. Many times, she used my own techniques on me and helped me see in myself the same patterns and learning curves that I so easily spot in others.

As a recovering people-pleasing perfectionist, I struggled to put my thoughts to paper and then let someone else criticize or dismiss what I have been applying and using instinctively since childhood. Jennifer's hours of research to back up scientifically what God had shown me as the way to approach fearful students was life-altering and helped me become a better teacher and writer. I am blessed to call her my friend. Together, we put in print what we want for everyone: the way to be fear free.

By Jennifer

My deepest gratitude goes to Laura Daley, who not only led me on the journey to riding fear free but who also trusted me to help her communicate her ideas to the horse world. She changed my life for the better, and I hope our book will help our readers as well.

For more information and support as you continue riding fear free, visit **www.RidingFearFree.com**.

You can also find us on....

Twitter

Riding Fear Free: http://twitter.com/RidingFearFree

Laura Daley: http://twitter.com/DaleyTLC

Jennifer Becton: http://twitter.com/JenniferBecton

Facebook

Riding Fear Free Book Page:
http://www.facebook.com/RidingFearFree

Riding Fear Free Support Group:
http://www.facebook.com/groups/RidingFearFree/

Jennifer Becton: http://www.facebook.com/JenniferBectonWriter

For more information about historical fiction and thrillers by Jennifer Becton, please visit http://www.bectonliterary.com or http://www.jwbecton.com.

Made in the USA
Middletown, DE
06 March 2020